Complete Works of Lokuang

Vol. 42

Essays on Chinese Philosophy

Student Book Co. LTD.

Contents

My Philosophy of Life

At the end of last year after the reviesed edition of my Philosophy of Life had been published, readers said that the arrangement was not as clear as that of the original version and that the content was much more difficult to understand. The arrangement was not as clear as that of the original version reason for this reaction is probably that in the revised version I dealt more with metaphysical ontology but did not go in to sufficient detail. Actually, the content of the revised version has a carefully organized inner arrangement but this arrangement is not too apparent on the surface. Therefore, I propose in this essay to put forth simply and clearly my system of thought.

I. The Confucian Philosophy of Life

Metaphysical onology in Western philosophy is based on the concept of "being", which is the fundamental concept for everything. This concept is the same as the expression we have in Chinese to call everything in the universe: wan-yu "Being" is the ultimate concept and it is also the very first one. Its meaning is very simply, we can only say "being" is truth, beauty and goodness. Its relationships are determined by the principled of identity, contradiction, and causality. This kind of explanation belongs to Western philosophy and theoretically can be used to investigate the essence of an object. "Being" itself however cannot be analyze but can only be described.

Chinese philosophy began with The Book of Changes, which is based on the concept of "change", the entire universe is "change". Each substance is "change". In fact, "being" in Western philosophy is the same as this "change", which is the "change" of yin and yang. All things become entitles through the change of yin and yang; yin and yang are continually in a state of change throughout the universe and continue to change within each thing becoming an entity. The Book of Changes calls this type of change "life". The entire universe is one life, and each thing also has its own life. Because of this, Chu hsi writes that "principle is one but its manifestations are many (li yi erh shu) (Chan 635). The universe has only a single life principle, yet each thing has its own life principle. Chu Hsi further says: " With respect to heaven and earth, there is the Great Ultimate in them. With respect to the myrid things, there is the Great Ultimate in each and every one of them" (Chan 638). This is because ch'i (vital force) is pure (ch'ing) and impure (chuo). Because of this difference, the vital force of yin and yang, in producing entities, causes the life produced from this principle of life to be different lives. Yin and yang are continually in motion in the universe, ever circulating, ever continuing life. The universe thus becomes the great flow of life.

The consant continuation of life in the universe manifests the virtue of Heaven and Earth to bring forth life. Chu Hsi writes, "The mind of Heaven and Earth is to produce things" (Chan 593). Producing things in benevolence (jen). Benevolence is thus life. The constant continuation of life in the universe is based on the inter-connectedness, mutual dependence, and mutual communication of all things. The life of man thus requires exchange between men, between things and men, and between men and nature. Therefore Confucius used benevolence as his unifying principle (yi kuan chih tao). Confucianism taked benevolence as the central principle of all goodness. For mutual exchange and mutual assistance, each thing should be in its proper place, which is yi (dutifulness). And its action should be appropriate to itself which is chung yung (the mean). Confucian philosophy uses these concepts as a systematic summary.

II. The Source of Life

Within the universe, everything is in motion. The highest type of motion is within the life of man. Within the life of man the highest part is the spirtual life. The spirit is formless and intelligent. In motion, it has neither shape nor image, an did limited to neither space nor time. Furthmore, the life of man does not have self-being, that is, existence from itself. The substance of other things of course also does not have self-being. Nor does the universe taken self-being. Therefore, life must have its own source.

All things in the universe are relative beings. The life of all things therefore is relative. The ceaseless change in the entire universe produces all things. Neither the ceaseless change in the universe nor its life have self-being. Rather, both come from an absolute life, which is the source of all life.

Absolute life is of course superior to the life of man and by necessity is pure spirit and perfect life. Whatever is proper to life is by necessity proper to the level of the absolute, which is absolutely without imperfection. Therefore it is absolute truth, beauty, and goodness.

Absolute life is also absolute "perfection", entirely without "potency". Moreover it is perfect "completion" and perfect "action" or "pure action" (actus purus). Therefore it has no change.

" Pure action " cannot be inanimate and unitelligent. Absolute spirit is by necessity the highest form of life. This type of changeless and motionless life, when seen from the perpective of our intellect, cannot be imagined because all concepts within our intellect are special and temporal. We cannot think of motion beyond time and space.

We use our intellect to think about this life that is highest and absolute. It lives within us because it is a unique entity. The life of pure spirit, according to the thought of our intellect, is as life of the intellect and will, absolute life knows itself and loves itself. Knowing itself, it must have an object of its knowledge. In myself, an idea is an idea, but in is an idea of itself. In myself, an idea is an idea, but in absolute life, it is absolute being. Its ideas are its substance. Similarly, if there is self-love, there is an obejct of one's love. The object is oneself and is one's idea of self. In absolute life, which is absolute being, the object one's love is one's substance. From our human perspective, the self-knowledge of absolute goodness. It cannot be enclosed within itself. If there is "self-love" there must be "love of the other". In as much as there is no substance beyond itself, it must use its "strength" to make "other substances". Absolute life creates using its own "strength" , which is absolute. Because it is "all-powerful", it has the "creative power" to make something out of nothing. What is created is the universe. The universe comes about through the creative power of absolute life; this creative power is living. The universe therefore connot be inanimate. It shares the life of absolute life. Therefore all the universe becomes a great flow of life.

The life of things in the universe is relative and material. It exists because of having been created by the creative power of absolute life. In order to continue "to exist", it must depend on the support of the creative power of absolute life. Otherwise it will immediately return to nothingness. In order to "move", it must depend on being placed in motion by the creative power of absolute life. Beyond its chemical qualities, each type of substance has its own qualities. Beyond its physical qualities each sbustance has its own strength and therefore can use its strength to take account of material things and designate them as objects. But each material thing does not have self-being. Nor is the strength which is given by absolute life to each material thing a kind of self-being which by absolute life to each material. Rather, the strength of a material thing, as its existence, must depend on the continual support of the creative power. Its power is motion, which also depends on the support of creative power St. Thomas called this kind of support continual creation. Furthermore, this so-called "continual", from the perspective of absolute life or absolute being, in as much as it transcends time and space, has only a now and only contemporaneity. It is without any of what is normally called "continual". In this way, the creative power of absolute life is the life of absolute life flowing throught the universe, flowing within all things. Thus there is change within the universe and within all things. This change is life.

III. Relavitve Life is the Change from Potency to Completion

Aristotle and St. Thomas speak of the change of all things in the universe, explaining it as going from "potency" to "complection". Because all things in the universe are relative beings, and do not have self-being, they cannot go from nothing to being, rather they go from being to being. The process of this change goes from a start to a finish.

The start is potency and the end completion. This process of going from start to finish is called action. For example, to read, I have to have the potential of knowing how to read. The activator of this potency to read is action, and only in this way can I read. When I read, the act of reading is accomplished. Reading is not just a single act. To continue to read, I continue to follow the act of reading from potency to completion, and lead a life of reading.

"Potency" belongs to "nature", "action" to "existence". Western philosophy speaks of "being" and explains it as having "nature" and "existence". "Nature" is the principle of "being", "Existence" is the actuality of "being". Being is formed of "nature" and "existence". The "potency" of each substance is determined by its proper nature. The "action" of a substance is determined by its actual existence. The action of going from "potency" to "completion" requires an activator. From the perspective of physics, the activator of a substance is its energy. It is either a positive or negative activator. The potential to move or to receive is "potency". Each thing either has the potency to move itself or to be moved by an outside force. According to what has been said above, this type of power has the potency to move itself or to be moved by an outside force. According to what has been said above, this type of power of action depends on the support of the absolute creative power. With the support of creative power, the power of action of a thing is also able to produce new life, thereby becoming a kind of "creative power". Because they have this type of creative power, all things in the universe can continue to reproduce, to progress, and to live. The change in all things is called life. Change is the action of going from potency to completion. Action is thus life.

The substance of life is a living thing. Life and a living things is not identical. Life's continual change is the continual change of a substance. Since a substance continues to change, where is the beginning and end of this change? What is the beginning and end of this change? The beginning and end is of course a substance. This question in Western philosophy is a question of "identity", that is, a question of "I". I am in continual change but the I change, I am still ever myself. Because who can say that the I of ten years ago is not the I of today.

Althought the substance and function of the I work together, they are not identical.

IV. The Wholeness of Life

Accordingly, the unity of substance comes from the unity of life. Life originally is not divisible. One year has my entire life. A second also has my entire life. It is like the soul in the body which is the entire soul, yet every small part of the body also has the entire soul. With a soul there is life; a soul cannot be divided, nor can life be divided. Life continues to change because only with change is life. It continues to form a unity because only in this way is there life. Once this continuance is divided, there is no longer continuance, there is no longer life. It is similar to the dure é of Bergson that cannot be divided. Division is not dure é.

The life of a substance cannot be divided because life is the actual existence of a substance. Whenever life is divided, the actual existence of a substance is destroyed and the substance no longer exists. The wholeness of a substance also comes about because of "actual existence". which is concrete existence, otherwise it would not be existence. For example, "nature" is whole and cannot be divided. As soon as it is divided, it is not complete. A man would then not be a man or a dog be a dog.

A substance becomes whole because of life. Although there is change, still it does not lose its substantiality. I am who I am because of life. I am a whole. Although I change over the years, my indivdual identity remains.

Likewise, all things in the universe are in change, this change is life. Each thing has the wholeness of life. The change in all things comes from absolute life, which is the creative power of absolute being. Because of this creative power, all things share in the life of absolute life. Creative power is one. The life bestowed by creative power is also one. But, even though the life received by all things in the universe is one life, it is nevertheless received on the basis of each things "nature". Because these "natures" are not the same, these lives are not the same. Therefore, Chu Hsi says, the principle is one but its manifestations many (li yi erh shu). The principle of life is identical but each thing receive it because of the vital force (chi) with which it is endowed. Vital force has the difference of pure (ching) and impure (chuo). Therefore, the principle of life for each thing is not same.

Although the life of all things is not the same, the life received is the one life given by the creative power. Therefore the life of the universe is one. And all things in the universe form a whole. Wang Yang-ming speaks of "the unity of benevolence".

Because there is a wholeness of life, all things in the universe are interrelated, inter-dependent and mutually communicating. Nothing in the universe can exist by itself. Whenever one part of the universe is harmed, all the other parts are also harmed. Therefore Confucianism uses "benevolence" to stand for "life". "Life" needs "love". Mencius wants men to be "benevolent towards the people and loving with all things" (II, 285) ! Nowadays, "environmental pollution" and "ecology" are confirmation of this idea.

V. The Consciousness of Life

Hegel once said that selfhood is the absolute spirit. The non-I is manifested through selfhood. When the non-I returns to the absolute spirit, then there is thesis, antithesis, and synthesis. The universe is the manifestation of the selfhood of the absolute spirit. When the universe returns to the absolute spirit, then man has religious consciousness, artistic consciousness and philosophical consciousness. Because man has these three types of consciousness, he is conscious that he is spirit. But this view is very circular. Actually, when the universe returns to absolute life, which is the creator, it all occurs within human consciousness.

Only man within all the things in the universe has consciousness. Consciousness not only is rational intelligence but also rational introspection. Within introspection, the power of rational speculation gives way to the power of intuition.

Consciousness of self-consciousness. Self-consciousness starts from external obsevation, observing exterior reality and observing the actions of the self. Then it progresses toward interior observation, reflecting about self and directly looking at one's existence, directly experiencing one's life.

With self-consciousness and introspection, I know what within the universe is knowable and unknowable for me. The unknowable does not exist for me. If all mankind did not know a substance, that substance would not exist for mankind. As for knowledge of external reality, it is not intuitive knowledge. But if it does not enter my intuitive consciousness, it does not enter into my life and does not become a part of my life, thereby not arriving at the condition of being "benevolent towards the people and loving with all things" (Mencius, II, 285).

All things within the universe are my knowledge, but they are not created by my rationality on the basis of nothing but are created on the basis of the matter of each being. My emotional life extends to exterior phenomenon and effects my rational life, thereby giving me an idea of external phenomena. External phenomena thus enter within my rational life. Then, these phenomena effect my intentional and emotional life in such a way that my love is infused into the phenomena I know. Love is "benevolence". Benevolence is the center of life. Because of love, my life is poured within the life of external phenomena, thereby allowing these two kinds of life to have mutual communication. Through the love within me, I am directly conscious of external phenomena because the structuring of this love is not dependent on reason but is directly absorbed by life. Within this type of consciousness, I am directly conscious of external phenomena. Although external phenomena are not rational and cannot have consciousness, nonetheless, within my consciousness, they gain a consciousness. Thus, through by consciousness, they can return to the origin of the creative power, praising the absolute life of truth, beauty and goodness.

VI. The Development of Life

For the sake of the great flow of life, my life cannot function only alone within me. It must be in touch with the life of the universe. As soon as I have life, I am immediately directly in contact with other lives, that is, the relationship I have with the life of my parents. Not only within the womb of my mother is my life inextricably bound with her life, but after birth, the development of my life is definitely mutually tied up with the life of my parents. The people in my family are thus the first circle within which starts the development of my life. Within a family, the life of all the members are inter-connected. Confucianism thus make filial piety as the basis of all virtues. Of the five Confucian relationships, three occur within the family.

After becoming an adult, the area for the development of my life extends to society. Mencius says, "Treat the aged of your own family in a manner befitting their venerable age and extend this treatment to the aged of other families; treat your own young in a manner befitting their tender age and extend this to the young of other families". My life is related to the life of people in society. In the Analects, it is written that "all within the Four Seas are brothers". The rule of benevolence — "Loving others as oneself" — is the right path for the path of my life within society and my nation. The Book of Rited speaks of the Great Unity (Ta-tung). Confucius says, " A benevolent man helps others to take their stand in so far as he himself wishes to take his stand, and gets others there is so far as he himself wishes to be there". The teachings of Jesus are contained within the expression "benevolent" love. St. John the Apostle says, "One who does not love his brother remains in death" (I John 3:14). Living occurs within human society and within the natural world. All things within the natural world are in mutual contact. The development of my life requires the assistance of the life of the natural world. My life must be connected to its life. The life of all things in the world is a single being. The life of man is the head of the whole of this life. The head needs to use every aspect of the body and every aspect of the depends on the head. Because of this relationship both have life. If the head uses its life to hurt any aspect of the body, to the extent of harming or destroying it, then the life of the head will receive injury. At present, environmental pollution harms things and harms man, abuse of natural resources violates the laws of "nature". The consumption of resources will also lead to the shortage of resources for man. The ancients in China taught man to be "benevolent towards the people and loving with all things" (Mencius II, 285).

Modern man takes full advantage of the opportunities before him. The eggs of black fish, as soon as they are laid, are taken to be caviar. A dish of caviar means the death of thousands of unborn fish. Now drift nets are being used for fishing; after a hundred years, the fish of the sea will become extinct. Many animals and birds have already become extinct. After fish become extince, man will be forced to eat man-made chemical products. The source of life will soon come to an end. Absolute created all things in the universe and put man in control. Man, however, kills and destroys life. If absolute life -- the creator -- does not send punishment, then natural law will react so that man will not be able to continue to exist. All things within the natural world and my life together form one wondrous circle. My life and the life of all things are inter-connected and natually linked. This inter-linking is not the concentration (chih kuan) of the Tien-tai and Hua-yen Schools of Buddhism, which is shown "the One enters everything, and everything enters the one enters everything, and everything enters the one." Rather, it the nature assistance of life. Does not the Confucian sage praise Heaven and Earth for nourishing a great man and uniting his virtue with Heaven and Earth.

VII. The Transcendence of Life

My life comes from absolute life. My life has self-consciousness. My self-consciousness is aware of my life's movement toward the eternal and my life's tendency to pursue the unlimited. Within my actual life, I pursue pleasure; pleasure accounts for the development of my life. Authentic pleasure will give my life authentic development. Wrong pleasure, on the other hand, will bring destruction to my life. In the pursuit of pleasure, I am often inclined to the unlimited. Some things to have even more of the better. The temporal span of my life is not knowable to me, which confirms the tendency of my life to the external and unlimted, and also confirms that my life comes from absolute life, which is enternal and unlimited because we share in the eternals and unlimited life of absolute life.

Ancient Chinese philosophy -- Confuscianism, Budddhism, and Taoism, all clearly pointed out that man's life should transcend the limited boundaries of earthly life. Taoism points out that man forgets the form and unites the original spirit of his mind with the original spirit of the universe to become a "holy man" (chen jen) and to live as long as the universe. In Chuang-tzu's parable, the holy man, traveling the universe, enters fire and does not burn, enters water and does not become wet.

Buddhism points out that man destroys his false mind to find his true mind. The true mind is the real self. The real self is the eternal (chen-ju), which is absolute substance. When man and the eternal is united, man enters nirvana, which is "eternity, bliss, personality and purity". Confucianism points out that man unites and intermingles with Heaven and Earth, praising all that Heaven and Earth have brought about. According to the "Commentaries" of the Book of Changes, "The great man accords in his character with heaven and earth; in his light, with the sun and moon; in his consistency, with the four seasons; in the good and evil fortune that he creates, with gods and spirits". Chinese philosophy consistently has advocated the spiritual life of man, developing it to the realm of the eternal and unlimited.

My life comes from absolute life and is united with the life of all things in the universe. I can be "benevolent towards the people and loving with all things" (Mencius II, 285). My life is linked with all things in the universe and has, according to Mencius, a "flood-like ch'i" (hao jan chih chi) (Mencius I, 57), which transends the universe and returns to absolute life, we are told, according to proverb, to "have the proper funeral rites for our parents and offer the appropriate sacrifices afterwards". Our beginning is in absolute life and so is our end.

My Catholic faith teaches me that my life's ultimate home is in returning to God, my creator, who is absolute, perfect life and absolute truth, beauty and goodness. In my return to God, my life gains eternal existence because His life is eternal. Because of His absolute truth, beauty and goodness, the joy that my life has been seeking for is finally achieved. The completion of my transcendent life is a transcendental, fully penetrating love because God is love and the life of absolute life is love.

In conclusion, allow me to cite from the revised version of my philosophy of Life.

Within love, a unity is formed. Transcendent life in Catholicism is not an impersonal life, nor is it a life that eliminates all emotion. It is not a superficial, empty life. Rather, it is an utterly real and alive transcendenet life. It is not a heavenly flight to an unapproachable God but it is the life of God within me. Transcendent life is the substance of life experiencing life itself. It is the unity of source of life with created life; it is man with his entire soul calling God "Father".

Works Cited

(1) Chan Wing-Tsit, trans. and comp. *A Source Book in Chinese Philosophy.* Princeton: Princeton UP, 1963.

(2) Confucius. *The Analects.* Trans. D.C. Lau Hong Kong: Chinese UP, 1979.

(3) *The I Ching or Book of Changes.* The Richard Wilheim translation rendered in English by Cary F. Baynes (1950). 3rd ed. Bolingen Series 19. Princeton: Princeton UP, 1967.

(4) Lo Kuang. *The philosophy of life.* Rev. ed. Taipei: Taiwan Hsueh-sheng, 1988.

(5) *Mencius.* Trans. D.C. Lau. 2 vols. Hong Kong: Chinese UP, 1984.

The Confucian Philosophy of Life

None of the Chinese thinkers of the past generations has ever written a book systematically presenting their own philosophy. The works that they have left behind are collections of sayings and essays. When we now study their thought, we must first seek the essential ideas in their sayings and essays, and then analyze and rearrange these ideas so as to present them systematically, remembering that a simple thought is premised on a simple system, a complex one on a comlex system. Furthermore, to establish that our research is not airy speculation without any foundation, we must continually refer to the original works of these thinkers.

Confucian thought is extermely complex, both in content and in origin. Accordingly, to discuss the system of Confucian thinking is a difficult scholarly enterprise. And, if we should leave the realm of objectivity, it would not be a scholarly enterprise.

I. A Metaphysical System

1. Follwing the Cosmic Order (fa-tien) Scholars in general say that Confucianism is moral philosophy, not metaphysics. But, in The Doctrine of the Mean, there is this passage:

> Therefore the Way of the true ruler is rooted in his own personal life and has its evidence (in the following) of the common people. It is tested by the experience of the Three Kings and found without error, applied before Heaven and Earth and found to be without contradiction in their operatioin, laid before spiritual beings without question or fear, and can wait a hundred generations for a sage (to confirm it) without a doubt. (Ch. 29, Chan III)

The kind of unchanging ethics presented in this passage can only be established on a metaphysical basis.

The basic principle of Confucian ethics is seen in the following two questions:

> Heaven creates divine things; the holy sage takes them as models. Heaven and earth change and transform; the holy sage imitates them. (The I Ching, "Ta Chuan/The Great Treatise", Part 1, Ch. 11, Wilhelm/Baynes 320)

> How lofty! It is Heaven that is great and it was Yao who modelled himself upon it. (The Analects, BK. 8, Ch. 19, Lau 73).

In The Book of History and The Book of Odes, the obejctive of following the cosmic order is know the will of Heaven. When the emperor and the people follow the decree of Heaven, they are following the cosmic order. In The Book of Changes, however, the intent of Heaven is expressed in the tao of heaven and earth. This tao is the rule for human life. How this tao functions in The Book of Changes is described as follows:

> The Changes is a book vast and great, in which everything is completely contained. The tao of heaven is in it, the tao of the earth is in it, and the tao of man is in it. It combines these three primal powers and doubles them; that is why there are six lines. The six lines are nothing other than the ways (tao) of the three primal powers. ("Ta chuan / The Great Treatise", Part 11, Ch. 10, Wilhelm / Baynes 351-352)

As for the The Doctrine of the Mean, it sees the tao of heaven in man. Man's nature thus represents the heavenly tao. If man lives according to his nature, he is following the cosmic order:

> What Heaven (T'ien, Nature) imparts to man is called human nature. To follow our nature is called the Way (Tao). Cultivating the Way is called education. (The Doctrine of the Mean, Ch. 1; Chan 98)

Wang Yang-ming considers conscience to be the heavenly tao of human nature. A conscience knows what is right without study. Even so naturally it can enlighten man as to the right or wrong of an action. If man can carry out his conscience and thus unite his knowledge and action, he is, for Wang Yang-ming, following the cosmic order.

Although the idea of following the cosmic order has undergone these changes, the basis of Confucian ethics is still always the heavenly tao of the universe.

2. Change in the Universe

The Book of Changes is the first Chinese philosophical work with a metaphysics. It describes the tao of change in the universe. The universe is seen as a unified body ever in change. Each thing within the universe is in constant change, too. The reason for his continual change is the elements of yin and yang found within each thing. Yang is active, hard, and positive. Yin passive, soft, and negative. These two elements are the basic components of ch'i (vital force), which is the fundamental constructive element of the universe. "The Great Treatise" of The Book of Changes comments:

> That which lets now the dark (yin), now the light (yang) appear is tao. As continuer, it is good. As completer, it is the essence. (Sec. 1, Ch. 5; Wilhelm/ Baynes 297-298)

The interplay of yin and yang causes continual change in the universe, and makes all things come to be and grow. In other words, each change in yin and yang constitutes the nature of a thing; and through this change, a thing goes on to exist.

The changes in yin and yang are circular, and ever alternating. The phenomenon of this change is always within time and space. Scholars of The Book of Changes in the Han Dynasty were the first to place the changes of yin and yang within time and space. By time is meant the year and its four seasons; by space, the four directions; north, south, east and west. The four seasons and four directions are matched depending on their yin and yang. Spring and east correspond: yang is becoming stronger, yin weaker. Summer is paired with south: yang is at its strongest; yin its weakest. Autumn goes with west: yang is becoming weaker, ying stronger. Winter corresponds to north: yin is at its strongest, yang its weakest. Adding the center to the four directions and mid-season to the four seasons, we then have a correspondence to the five elements; metal, wood, water, fire and earth. The seasons are in continual change, and so are the yin and yang of universe.

3. Within Time

The yin and yang of the four seasons, moreover, have a strong and weak point that occur at the appropriate time. This regularity allows for the harmony of the change in the universe. In the eyes of ancient Chinese, this harmony is manifested by the favorable weather.

In the hexagrams in The Book of Changes, the second and fifth line of each hexagram is considered the mean (chung). It is the most important position in each hexagram. Each hexagram is constructed of lines representing either yin or yang. Each kind of line has its own appropriate place, which is called its proper position (cheng). When a line in its appropriate place in the middle, it is said to be in its mean and proper (chung cheng) position. The mean and proper (chung cheng) signifies that things within space and time have their appropriate position, and also expresses the harmony of the universe.

Each things, when it has its proper harmony, has the yin and yang appropriate to its mean and proper (chung cheng). If a thing is not internally harmonious, it has a negative influence on the harmony of the universe. For instance, in ancient times, marriages were arranged on the basis of the date and time of the birth of the man and woman. The moment of birth was supposed to have been determined by the coming together of yin and yang. From this coming together of yin and yang was thought to arise the interaction of the five elements with their predetermined order of precedence. When the dates and times of birth for the man and woman to be marrried were placed together, it should then have become clear whether their marriage would be mutually supportive or mutually destructive. Depending on the interaction of the five elements of the couple, it would be decided whether or not the couples should marry.

4. Begetter of All Begetting (sheng sheng)

The changes in the universe have a lofty purpose: the begetting of all things. The elements of change in the universe are both in the heavens and on the earth. In the heavens these elements are celestial phenomena such as the sun, the moon, wind, frost, rain and dew; on the earth, they include natural phenomena such as mountains, rivers, water and earth. These celestial and natural phenomena must be in harmoney for the begetting of all things. In the lives of farmers in ancient China, each natural phenomenon was related to the raising of crops. The seasons, and especially the weather, were the most closely related to farming.

Change is explained in this way in The Book of Changes:

> As begetter of all begetting it is called change. (Ta Chuan/The Great Treatise", Part 1, Ch. 5 Wilhelm/Baynes 299).

The reason for change in the universe is to put in motion the begetting of all things; thus this begetting is both the very change in the universe and the object of it. This ideas expressed clearly in the following passages:

> It is the virtue of heaven and earth to bestow life. (The I Ching, "Ta Chuan/The Greate Treatise", Part II, Ch. 1; Wilhelm/ Baynes 328)

> Heaven and stimulate each other, and all things take shape and come into being. (The I Ching, Shien Hexagram, "Commentary on the Decision"; Wilhelm/Baynes 541)

> Does Heaven Speak? The four seasons pursue their courses, and all things are continually being produced. (The Analects, Bk. 17, Ch. 19, Lau 177)

> Heaven and earth have no other purpose than the bringing into being of things. The basic vital force revolves and circulated

without end. It just begets the innumberable things of the universe. (Classified Conversations of Chu Hsi, chiian 1)

Confucian thinkers have continuously taken celestial and earthly changes as the basis for the begetting of all things. This process is intentional and is called cosmic vertue. Lao tzu has said that if heaven and earth are without benevolence (jen), the begetting of things is blind natural movement. For a Confucian, heaven and earth are purposeful because, at the bottom, he believes in Heaven or God. Heaven and earth are the external manifestation of divine action.

The universe is a totality through which life massively flows. This principle of life is within each object, but it has different ways of manifesting itself. In minerals, this life is a hidden and unmanifested inanimate entity. In the various kinds of plants and animals, life is manifested in degrees. The fullness of life is shown in man. Chu Hsi says that within heaven and earth all things have the same principle of life, but it is shown in different ways. Man's life is the most complete, and, the highest life for man is that of the spirit.

Within life, man, things in heaven, and those on earth are mutually related, forming a triad. Wang Yang-ming speaks of "the benevolence of the totality". To maintain life, man must eat meat and vegetables, and even minerals in medicine. Within life, man is not isolated.

All things within the universe have life. This idea is presented in Chinese proetry and painting. In Poetry, the sun, the moon, flowers and trees all have feelings. In painting, mountains and streams, grass and woods all have life. And the life within a painting is always harmonious.

II. Ethical System

Man is a part of the universe. Man's life and the life of all things are related. The tao for man is that for change in the universe. Man should imitate the comsic virtues so that the tao of heaven and earth will also be the tao for man.

Not every man can understand the tao of heaven and earth; only the sage. In Confucianism, some men are born sages, others become sages through discipline. The unspoiled heart of a sage by birth has no harmful desire and is at peace with heaven and earth. He understands the principle of the changes for heaven and earth, and, according to this principle, acts properly, teaches and governs. Although the hexagrams of The Book of Changes can be seen as superstition, in ancient times they represented an ethical thought to be used to govern men. Hexagrams were created by sages and commentaries on them written by sages. "The Great Treatise" of The Book of Changes describes this process:

> Therefore, with respect to the images: The holy sages were able to survey all the confused diversities under heaven. They observed forms and phenomena, and made representations of things and their attributes. These were called the Image. The holy sages were able to survey all the movements under heaven. They contemplated the way in which these movements met and became interrelated, to take their course according to eternal laws. Then they appended judgments, to distinguish between the good fortune and misfortune indicated, these were called the Judgements. The exhaustive presentation of the confused diversities under heaven depends upon the hexagrams. The stimulation of all movements under heaven depends upon the Judgments. The transformation of things and the fitting together of them depend upon the changes. Stimulation of them and setting them in motion depend upon continuity. The spirituality and clarity depend upon the right man. Silent fulfillment, confidence that needs no words, depend upon virtuous conduct. (Part 1, Ch. 12; Wilhelm/Baynes 324)

Through the hexagrams and their commentaries, which can be used as a principle of governing, sages express the change that they have observed in the universe and in the tao. In The Book of Changes, sage is one with the virtue of heaven and earth and follows the order of the four seasons:

When he acts in advance of heaven, heaven does not contradict him. When be follows heaven, he adapts himself to the time of heaven. ("Chien Hexagram", "The Commentaries", Wilhelm/Baynes 328-383)

1. Man's Nature

Although the sages invented the hexagrams and wrote their commentaries so as to govern men, on the natural level, man has the tao, which is called the principle of heaven, in his heart from birth. This principle in man's heart is called the nature of man. If man lives according to the tao of heaven and earth, he is living according to his own nature, the principle of heaven. According to The Doctrine of the Mean, What Heaven (Tien, Nature) imparts to man is called human nature. To follow our nature is called the Way (Tao). Cultivating the Way is called education" (Ch. 1; Chan 98). Man's nature is thus the norm of his life and it is also the principle of heaven.

In the view of Mencius, the principle of heaven regarding man's nature is benevolence (jen), dutifulness (yi), observance of rites (li) and wisdom (chih 智). At birthman possesses these four virtues. Because man at birth also has a heart of compassion, a heart of shame, a heart of courtesy and modesty, and a great of right and wrong, his life should be devoted to developing the above-mentioned virtues (Mencius, BK. 2, Part A, Ch. 6; Lau 67). This concept is Mencius doctrine of man's virtuous nature.

Hsun-tzu, on the other hand, sees man's nature as evil. At birth man possesses an aggressive and selfish heart. On the basis of the teachings of the sages, man must exert himself to correct his evil nature so as to virtuous and good. Therefore, goodness in man is acquired.

Confucianists of the Han and Tang Dynasties divided man's nature into 3 classes or 5 classes. Some men are sages by birth; others at birth are evil-doers; yet others are in the middle, capable of both good and evil. Neither Mencius, Husn-tzu nor Han and Tang Confucianists, however, have pointed out the root of good and evil. Chu hsi, in his philosophical thought, has answered this question. Man's nature originally has the principle of heaven, but is without any good or evil, because the nature of heaven and earth is without good or evil. Each person, moreover, has his own individual nature, which is composed of principle (li) and vital force (chi). The principle is the principle of heaven and is the same for all men. Vital force can be either clear or spotted. If is clear, then the individual nature is good; if spotted, evil. However, since Chu hsi used ontology to explain the nature of good and evil in ethics, thus mixing together ontology and ethics, he did not resolve the question. Furthermore, Ching Dynasty Confucianists Yen yuan and Li kung possed this idea.

No matter how we look at the problem of whether man's nature is good or evil, Confucian philosophers have consistently maintained that man's nature is the ethical norm. The Great Learning speaks of "manifesting a clear character" (ming ming-te). The Doctrine of the Mean seeks to establish a sincere (chih cheng) personality. And, Wang Yang-ming advocated following one's conscience (chih liang chih); when man wants to act, conscience shows him the principle of heaven, so that man will know the right or wrong of this action and, accordingly, decide whether to do it or not.

2. The Doctrine of the Mean

Within the changes of the universe, everything has its own proper place. These changes therefore are harmonious. Man's action also has its proper place, which is called the "Mean".

> Before the feelings of pleasure, anger, sorrow, and joy are aroused it is called equilibrium (chung), centrality, mean. When these feelings are aroused and each and all attain due measure and degree, it is called harmony....(When equilibrium and harmony are realized to the highest degree, heaven and earth will attain their proper order and things will flourish. (The Doctrine of the Mean, Ch, 1; Chan 98)

"Due measure and degree" brings about equilibrium and harmony, and is the harmonious movement of heaven and earth that allows all things to grow and develop. "Due measure and degree" has its proper time and place, and so is called moderation. Moderation is the tao of every day life. "Due measure and degree" should be related with everyday life. Take as an example filial piety. The equilibrum a rich and poor man should exhibit is not the same. A richman should honor his parents lavishly, a poor man simply.

To achieve "due measure and degree", Confucius supports the keeping of the rites (shou-li). He told Yen yuan: "Do not look unless it is in accordance with the rites; do not listen unless it is in accordance with the rites; do no speak unless it is accodance with the rites; do not move unless it is in accordance with the rites." (The Analects, BK. 12, Ch. 1: Chan 109). The kingly sage establishes the rites according to the principle of heaven. The Book of Rites says, "The sages have established the rites on the basis of the principle of heaven and earth" (Li Yun).

Sincere the rites are based on the principle of heaven, one who is not a sage would not dare to perform them. The Doctrine of the Mean says:

> Although a man occupies the throne, if he has not the corresponding virtue, he dare to institute systems of music and ceremony (rites). Although a man has the virtue, if he does not occupy the throne, he may not dare to institute systems of music and ceremony (rites) either. (Ch. 28; Chan 111)

The rites are the norm for action and give order to man's activity. For sacrifical ceremonies and for weddings and funerals, the participants take their place according to the ritual regulations. Then, each act is done in an order according to the rite. Rites thus have hierarchy and order. Music, on the other hand, allows each sound to combine into a harmonious melody, hence the expression "the voices may be different but the sound is one." Music also unites the hearts of men. Confucianism emphasizes rites and music. One separates men, the other unites them. Together they make the mean in men's actions:

> Confucius said, "Perfect is the Mean. For a long time few

people have been able to follow it." (The Doctrine of the Mean, Ch. 3; Chan 99)

The Chinese people, since the time of Emperors Yao and Shun, have been observing the doctrine of the mean. Because extremes are loathed, peace is loved.

3. Filial Piety

Life is an immense current in the universe. On the level of man, life has an ideal manifestation, and human life is the most precious of all life. It is handed down through the union of a man and woman. Marriage is the foundation of this union and is the great event of human life. Here is an interpretation of marriage in The Book of Changes:

> Commentary on the Decision: The marrying maiden describes the great meaning of heaven and earth. If heaven and earth do not unite, all creatures fail to prosper. The marrying maiden means the end and beginning of humanity.

> (" Kwei Mei Hexagram "; Wilhelm/Baynes 664)

> In The Book of Rites, it is said;

> If heaven and earth are not united, nothing will be begotten. Marriage makes for generations of property. (Chung-kung wen)

Through marriage comes the family, which is the basis of Chinese society and also the basis of life. Marriage joins the life of a person to that of this ancestors. A symbol of this continuity of life is honoring one's ancestors. This ceremnoy is chiefly done by the male heir, the eldest son, and symbolized that the life of the ancestors continues on. If man has no son, the chain is broken; his life comes to an end as does the life handed on to him by his ancestors. Mencius says, "there are three ways of being a bad son. The most serious is to have no heir" (Mencius, BK. 4, Part A, Ch. 26, Lau 155).

Birth is at the basis of Confucian filial piety. Because of the continuity of life, father and son are united. The son's body bears the remains of his parents. Receiving life from his parent, a son should be filial to his parents; and, carrying on this life, he should act so that each action is premised on filial piety. Unvirtuous conduct is unfilial.

In The Book of Rites, Tesng-tzu says, "There are three kinds of filial piety. The highest is honoring one's parents. The second highest is not to disgrace them; the third, taking care of them" (Chi yi). These three kinds of filial piety are the actions of a son during his lifetime. Even the emperor, who is considered the son of heaven, also must be filial. His filiality is of the highest type because he honors heaven in as much as heaven is seen as his parents. Homes often have a tablet honoring "Heaven, Earth, the Emperor, Parents and Teachers." Heaven and earth are the ultimate source of life. The Emperor, protecting the life of this people, represents Heaven. Parents, however, are the immediate source of life. Teachers instruct men in how to makes good use of life. The virtues of a family are thus all premised on the meaning of life. Filial piety thus becomes; "the foundation of virtue and the root of civilization" (The Hsiao Ching, Ch. 1).

4. Benevolence

Although Confucius emphasizes filial piety, he stresses benevolence even more. The Doctrine of the Mean says that benevolence "is the distinguishing characteristic of man" (Ch. 20; Chan 104).

What is the meaning of benevolence? Chu hsi says, "Love is not benevolence but benevolence is the principle of love. The heart is not benevolence, but benevolence is the virtue of the heart" (Classified Conversations, Chiian 20).

If benevolence is the principle of love, what is it that should be loved? Because one has his own life, life is what should be loved. If ones own life is loved, then the life of other people and other things will be love, too. For Chu hsi, benevolence is life: The basic meaning of life is benevolence" (Classified Conversations, Chiian 6).

Existence within heaven and earth is called "life" (sheng). Benevolence is the virtue of heaven and earth loving life. When there is benevolence, there is life. In traditional Chinese medicine, when it is said that the extremities are so numb that they have no benevolence (pu jen), it means that they are so numb that there is no life, In the Chinese expression for:"peach seed" and "apricot seed", the character for benevolence is used because of its meaning of "life-giving".

Living things, that is, benevolence, are at the heart of heaven and earth, Man is the most spirited part of things; his heart is the heart of heaven and earth, so it is a heart of benevolence. In the words of Chu Hsi:

> Begetting all things is at the great of heaven and earth, but at the heart of the heaven and earth is the begettig of man. Thus, regarding the virtue of the heart, although it embraces all things, in a word, it is nothing but benevolence, (Jen Chuo, Collection of Literary Works, Chuuan 67)

Man's heart is naturally benevolent. Therefore Mencius says, "Benevolence is the heart of man" (BK. 6, Part A, Ch. 11, Lau 235). And The Doctrine of the Mean states "benevolence is the destinguishing characteristic of man" (Ch. 20, Chan). Man naturally loves his life, the source of his life, and his parents. And he also naturally loves those connected with his life.

By loving one's life, one develops it. The life of man's soul is at the center of his life. Mencius regarded human nature to be benevolent; therefore, he wanted to develop the benevolence of man's nature. Confucius said, "(....a benevolent man) helps others to take their stand in so far as he himself wishes to take his stand, and gets others there in so far as he himself wishes to get there" (The Analects, BK. 6, Ch. 28, Lau 55). The benevolence that allows one to take a stand and help others to do so has the same significance that sincerity does in The Doctrine of the Mean:

> Only those who are absolutely sincere can fully develop their nature. If they can fully develop their nature, they can then

fully develop the nature of others. If they can fully develop the nature of others, they can then fully develop the nature of things. If they can fully develop the nature of things, they can then assist in the transforming and nourishing process of Heaven and Earth. (Ch. 22, Chan 107)

The highest purpose of the Confucian philosophy of life is to praise the development of heaven and earth. Here is how The Doctrine of the Mean praises Confucius:

He may be compared to earth in its supporting and containing all things, and to heaven in its over shadowing and embracing all things. He may be compared to the four seasons in succession, and to the sun and moon in their alternate shining. All things are produced and developed without injuring one another. The courses of the seasons, the sun, and moon are pursued without conflict. The lesser forces flow continuously like river currents, while the great forces go silently and deeply in their mighty transformations, it is this that makes heaven and earth so great. (Ch. 30, Chan 111)

Heaven and earth are great; sages are also great because they can praise the development of heaven and earth.

Furthermore, because of this idea, Confucianism has the concept of Great Unity (ta-tung), according to which, all men on earth are brothers. Man should not only love himself and his family but also extend this love to other men and their families. This doctrine is called universal love.

Because man's life is related to the life of all things in the universe, man's love should extend to all things. Chang tai in his essay "Hsi Ming" writes, "Men are my fellow creatures, and things are of my own kind, too." Wang Yang-ming, in his "Questions on The Great Learning", advocates "the benevolence of the totality." Man and things from the perspective of life form a unity; man should also love things. Mencius has said, "Benevolent men love all things."

With this sprit of the Great Unity, man can be fully happy. Mencius says: All the ten thousand things are there in me. There is no greater joy for me than to find, on self examination, that I am true to myself. Try your best to others as you would wish to be treated yourself, and you will find that this is the shortest way to benevolence. (BK. 7, Part A, Ch. 4, Lau 265)

When man loves all things, all things are included within his heart. In this way, means heart will be connected with the heart of heaven, reaching the stage of union between heaven and earth. Man's thoughts should not be only on his own self but on the totality of the universe. Fan Chung-yan has said: "Worry about the worries of others before they do, then be happy over their happiness after they are." A heart without personal worries often has the spirit of active love for others. President Chiang Kai-shek has said, "Take the rise and fall of all as your responsibility; place your own life or death outside your concern". All things of heaven and earth are within me. We live and die within the realm of heaven and earth. Jesus, sacrificing himself to save mankind so that those saved may have eternal life, also represents the benevolent Great Unity spirit of Confucianism.

Confucian philosophy has a systematic philosophy of life. Twentieth-century Western philosophy for the most part emphasizes life. Evolutionism, behaviorism, vitalism, utilitarianism, existenialism all study questions of life. Confucian philosophy not only studies the questions of life, but also systematically explain man's life, giving man a complete concept about how to develop his life.

Works Cited

(1) Confucius, *The Analects* (Lun Yu), Trans, D. C. Lau., Hong Kong: Chinese UP, 1983.

(2) *The Doctrine of the Mean, Trans.*, Wing-tsit Chan, A Source Book in Chinese Philosophy, Trans., and comp., Wing-tsit Chan, Princeton: Princton UP, 1963. p.95-114.

(3) *The I Ching or Book of Changes*, The Richard Whilelm translation rendered in English by Cary F. Baynes (1950), 3rd ed., Bollingen Series 19, princeton; Princeton UP, 1967.

(4) *Mencius*, Trans., D. C. Lau., 2 vols, Hong Kong: Chinese UP, 1984.

Chu Hsi's Theory of Metaphysical Structure

I. Introduction

In the history of Chinese philosophy, there is no term for metaphysics. There is only the term hsing-shang, of which scholars throughtout the centuries have had different interpretations. The terms hsing-erh-shang (prior to physical form) and hsig-erh-hsia (posterior to physical form) originally are derived from the I-ching (Book of Changes). According to its "Appended Remarks," "That which is hsing-erh-shang is called the Way (Tao); that which is hsing-erh-shia is called a concrete thing (ch'i). " [1] The Book of Changes did not give explanation or interpretation to these two terms; neither did scholars devoted to the study of the Classics in the Han Dynasty (206 B.C.-A.D. 220) pay much attention to these two sentences.

Han K'ang-po (332-380) commented on the sentence from the "Appended Remarks" part 1, chaper 2, "That which is visible we than call hsiang (form). That which has form we then call ch'i." [2] Han's commentary reads: "That which becomes form is called a concrete thing." [3] He takes hsing-erh-shang as that which does not yet have form and hsing-erh-hsia as that which has form.

Hsun Shuang's (128-190) commentary explained the sentence in question as follows: "It is said that the sun, moon, and stars that manifest themselves in the heavens become hsiang. The myriad things produced and grown on the earth have form and can be taken as concrete things."[4] Han K'ang-po's comment is based on this explanation, but neither Han nor Husn commented on the terms hsing-erh-shang and hsing-erh-hsia.

---

(1) *Book of Changes*, "Appended Remarks," pt. 1, Ch. 12.
(2) Ibid., Ch. 11.
(3) Han's commentary is found in the Thirteen Classics edition.
(4) Comment on Ibid.

Finally, in the Sung Dynasty (960-1279) scholar of the school of Principle (Li-hsueh) who studied principle (li) and material force (ch'i) began to pay attention to the problem of hsing-erh-shang and hsing-erh-hsia.

Chang Tsai's (1020-1077) I-shuo (Commentary on the Book of Changes) took hsing-erh-shang as a formless body and hsing-erh-hsia as a body with form. He said:

> Hsing-erh-shang is that which is formless. Therefore hsing-erh-shang is called the Way. Hsing-erh-hsia is that which has form. Therefore hsing-erh-hsia is called a concrete thing. That which has no form or leaves no trace is the Way, like great virtue which strengthens moral ties between humans. That which has form and leaves traces is a concrete thing, visible form fact and reality, like ceremony and etiquette, All that which is hsing-erh-shang is called the Way. Only because of this is it difficult to understand the connection between the point which divides being (yu) and nonbeing (wu) and physical form (hsing) and formlessness (wu-hsing). It is at this crucial point that material force begins. Therefore that which is material force can unite being and nonbeing. Out of nonbeing material force naturally arises. This is the Way and the Change. [5]

The opinions of Ch'eng I (Ch'eng-ch'uan, 1033-1107) and Ch'eng Hao (Ch'eng Ming-tao, (1032-1085) differ from Chang Tsai's opinion: "Tzu-hou (Chang Tsai) takes ch'ing-hsu-i-ta (the one great pure vacuity) to mean the Way of Heaven (Tien tao). Therefore he considers it not from the viewpoint of hsing-erh-shang, but from concrete things,"[6] In Chang Tsai's thinking, formlessness is hsing-erh-shang. And because he advocated that the material force of the

---

(5) I-shuo, 11:15b-16a, in the Chang Tzu ch'uan-shu *(Complete works of Chang Tsai),* (SPPY ed.).

(6) I-shu *(Surviving works),* 11:1b, in the Erh-Ch'eng ch'uan-shu (Complete works of the two Ch'engs), (SPPY ed.) The text does not mention Chang Tsai specifically, but the reference is clearly implied, for no one else but Chang Tsai had said that.

Grat Vacuity is formless material force it follows the material force of the Great Vacuity (T'ai-hsu) is hsing-erh-shang. As Chang noted: "Material force originated from vacuity, and therefore it sould originally be formless. Having been affected, it was produced. Thus congregating, it became form (hsiang)."[7] Ch'eng I and Ch'eng Hao did not agree with Chang's taking material force as hsing-erh-shang; moreover, the Way which is formless and the concrete thing which has form cannot exist in the same physical body. Therefore, that which has form and that which does not have form cannot explain hsing-erh-shang and hsing-erh-hsia. Even if material force is the material force of the Great Vacuity, it is still hsing-erh-hsia.

Chu Hsi follows what Ch'eng I and Ch'eng Hao advocated, He takes hsing-erh-shang as "prior or physical form" and hsing-erh-hsia as posterior to physical form. These two can coexist in the same object.

> That which is prior to physical form refers to principle. That which is posterior to physical form refer to facts and things."[8]
>
> Someone asked, "Why do you explain hsing-erh-shang and hsing-erh-hsia in terms of shang and hsia?"
>
> Chu Hsi replied, "Because it is most appropriate. Suppose you use 'form' and 'formlessness'. Then you sever the relationship of things and principle. Therefore when you use shang and hsia to describe the difference clearly, you are only drawing a clear distinction, not separating them from each other. A concrete thing is also the Way. The Way is also a concrete thing. They are distinct but not separate." [9]

The difference between Chu Hsi and Chang Tsai consists Chang Tsai's taking the constituting material force of the Great Vacuity as

---

(7) Cheng-ment *(Correcting youthful ignorance)*, Ch. 1.

(8) Chu Tzu yu-lei, *(Classified conversations of Master Chu)*, (Taipei Ch'eng-chung Book Co. 1970), 75:20a, p.3077.

(9) Ibid., 75:19b, p.3067.

formless, while Chu Hsi takes anything that has material force as hsing-erh-hsia.

> In heaven and earth there are principle and material force. Principle is the Way which is prior to physical form, the root of the creation of things. As for material force, it is the constitutive-elements of what is posterior to physcial form. It is the implement of the creation of things. For this reason the creation of man and things has to possess this principle and then there is the nature (hsing). It has to possess this material force, and then there is physcial form (hsing). [10]

> Hsing-shang and hsing-hsia merely refer to the separation, fusion, and distinction of form. This is precisely the point of demarcation. If you merely say "executing prior to" or "existing posterior to", then that separated them into two separate entities. [11]

In the beginning of the Ch'ing Dynasty (1644-1912), Wang Fu-chil had his own opinion on hsing-shang and hsing-hsia. He used "hidden" (yin) and "manifest" (hsien) to interpret these two terms.

The Way which is hidden is not nonexistence. Then how can it be found in the vast emptiness? That which is hsing-erh-shang is hidden; that which is hsing-erh-hsia is manifest. As soon as you speak the term hsing-erh-shang, you presuppose there is the word hsing (physical form) which leaves a trace that can be followed and can be referred to. [12]

> That which is formless is the darkness which cannot be seen by man. Formlessness is not really formless. Man's eyesight is

---

(10) Chu Tzu wen-chi, *Collection of literary works of Master Chu*, (SPPY ed. enti tled Chu Tzu ta-ch'uan, Complete collection of Master Chu, 58:4b, first reply to Huang Tao-fu.

(11) Chu Tzu yu-lei, 94:4a, p.3761.

(12) Tu Ssu-shu ta-chuan shuo, *On reading the Great Completion of the Four Books*, Ch. 2, commenting on the Doctrine of the Mean, Ch. 11.

circumscribed by the obscurity, so it is seen as obscure, The capacity of the mind is circumscribed by the vastness of what it contemplates. The power of eyesight and hearing are circumscribed by minuteness. [13]

Wang Fu-chih takes the Great Ultimate (T'ai-chi) as the material force of the Great Harmony (T'ai-ho). The material force of the Great Harmony already possesses yin (passive cosmic force) and yang (active cosmic force), but it is not yet manifest because there is no material force prior to yin and yang. If there is material force, yin and yang exist. The material force of the Great Human is then the material of which yin and yang are not yet made manifest. Human eyesight can not perceive yin and yang; therefore they are labeled as formless. When the two material forces of yin and yang are made manifest, then they are said to have form.

Tai Chen (1723-1777) of the Ch'ing Dynasty had another opinion. He thought that formlessness and having form should refer to "prior to form" and "posterior to form." "Form refer to the entity which has already become concrete. Hsing-erh-shang is like sayig prior to form and hsing-erh-hsia is like saying posterior to form. The yin yang that has not become an entity with form is said to be hsing-erh-shang. It is clear that it is not hsing-erh-hsia." [14]

The School of Principle explains hsing-shang and hsing-hsia by using the terms "having form" and "becoming form" and "mainfesting form." These are all based on material force. If material force is the only element comprising the universe and the myriad things in it, and if the distinction between hsing-shang and hsing-hsia is based on material force, then material force is either concrete or not yet concrete. That which is concrete is yin yang, is "posterior to form. That which is not yet concrete is hsing-erh-shang. Wang Fu-chih divided the

---

(13) Cheng-meng chu, Commentary on the Cheng-meng, p.12, in the Ch'uan-shan-i-shu *Surviving works of Wang Fu-chih*, (Taipei: Tzu-yu, Press, 1972).

(14) Meng Tuz tzu-i shu-cheng (Commentary on the meaning of terms in the Book of Mencius), in Hu Shih, Tai Tung-yuan ti che-hsuch (The philosophy of Tai Chen), (Shanghai: Commerical Press, 1972), sec, 17, p.73.

substance of material force into yin and yang. There is no material force that is not divided into yin and yang. He distinguished between hsing-erh-shang and hsing-erh-hsia in terms of the "hidden" and "manifest". Chu Hsi advocated the dualism of principle and material force. He took principle to be that which is hsing-erh-shang and material force as that which is hsing-erh-hsia, It seems to me that Chu Hsi's interpretation is closer to that which the "Appended Remarks" of the Book of Changes referred to as hsing-erh-shang and hsing-erh-hsia. The "Appended Remarks" takes the Way as hsing-erh-shang and concrete things as hsing-erh-hsia. The Way, we can say, is equal to principle, but we cannot say it is equal to the material force of the Great Vacuity. When we say principle is hsing-erh-shang, we mean that hsing-erh-shang is called the Way.

In Chinese philosophy we translate Aristotle's First philosophy as hsing-shang-hsueh, but we cannot take hsing-shang as the object of the study of First philosophy metaphysics. The metaphysics of Aristotle researches the highest principle or the ultimate principle of everything. The highest principle of every thing is the first principle of everything. Therefore, Western metaphysics studies "Being". Being is the substance of everything. Metaphysics studies the substance.

II. On Substance

Western ontology studies "Being" in the aspect of "Being" as an idea. "Being" is the simplest idea. It has the least intentional or connotative meaning. It can be neither analyzed nor explained. We can explain "Being" in terms of its character and its relationships. Truth, beauty, and goodness are the characteristics of Being; the law of identity, the law of contradiction, and the law of causality are its ontological relationships.

Ontology in the Book of Changes studies the metamorphosis of "being", that is, it studies the concrete "existence" of being becoming (ch'eng) or actus (hsing). Becoming or actus is the metamorphosis (hua). Metamorphosis was called change in the Book of Changes. I means change and change means metamorphosis (hua-sheng) or production by the perpetual renewal of life (sheng-sheng).

Things that are produced by metamorphosis are becoming or actus; they are also existence. On the perpetual renewal of life, the Book of Changes states that form the Great Ultimate, yin and yang are produced. From yin and yang, the Four Phenomena (ssu-hsiang) or the five Agents (wu-hsing)[15] are produced. Form the Four Phenomena or the Five Agents are produced things, which are "existence." Ontology in the Book of Changes is an ontology of actus. It studies actus. It is a philosophy of actus.

Although Chu Hsi's ontology studies production by metamorphosis and the perpetual renewal of life, he pays more attention to the structure of things as things. He analyzed things and advocates that things contain two elements, principle and material force. In Western philosophy, things fall within the boundary of cosmology. Both Aristotle and St. Thomas Aquinas advocated that things contained forma and materia. "Being" in ontology of course is hsing-shang, because it has no physical form; things belong to hsing-hsia because they have matter. The subject of ontology in Western philosophy is "Being", therefore it is certainly the science of hsing-shang. The subject of Western cosmology is "things"; therefore it is certainly the science of hsing-hsia. But since the ontology of both the Book of Changes and Chu Hsi studies material force as its subject, therefore it cannot but the science of hsing-hsia, but the substance of things belongs to the field of the science of hsing-shang. Therefore the ontology of the Book of Changes and Chu Hsi should be viewed as the science of hsing-shang-hsueh (metaphysics).

Although the terms of t'i (substance) and yung (function) appeared in philosophical thought before the Sung Dynasty, they were not in widespread use. These two terms were in common use in Buddhist scriptures and commentaries on the scriptures. The scholars of the School of principle in the Sung, Ming (1368-1644), and Ch'ing Dynasties were much influenced by Buddhist thought and widely used these two terms.

---

(15) Metal, Wood, Water, Fire, and Earth. Wu-hsing has also been translated as "Five Elements."

Chu Hsi discussed substance and function on many occasions, but his discussions on the substance of things are few. In discussing substance and function he focused for the most part on facts and events:

> What one should do is called substance. What one does is called function. For example, a fan consists of the spine, handle, and paper. This is substance. Fanning it is function. Another example is a ruler and a scale which has lines and dots. These are substance. We use them to measure and weight things. That is function. [16]

The substance in question is the subject, the function in question is the usage. There are many elements in the subject. Some of them belong to substance; some of them belong to accident:

> The spines of the fan themselves are substance. The flow or stagnancy of water or the waves of the water are function. The water itself can flow or be stagnant, can be stirred up into waves. This is substance.

Take for example, our body. It is substance. Seeing with the eyes and hearing with the ears and moving with the limbs are function. Or take the hand. It is substance, and pointing and carrying and other movements of the fingers are function. [17]

This substance means subjectum. The accident of the subjectum is function. But when Chu Hsi discussed the substance of things, he used Way or principle to refere to substance. He said:

> Substance is the principle and function is the usage, like the seeing of the eyes and the hearing of the ears. It is naturally so. This is principle. We use our eyes to see things. We use ears to hear sounds. That is function. [18]

---

(16) Chu Tzu yu-lei, 6:3a, p.163.
(17) Ibid., 6:2b, p.162.
(18) Ibid., 6:2b-3a, pp.162-163.

Someone asked. "Are substance and function always different?" Chu Hsi replied. "Take this signpost. It is one principle. It points out a direction down the road this way or that way. Or take house. It is one principle. It has sitting rooms and halls. There are Chang San and Li Ssu. Li Ssu can't be Chang San. Chang San can't be Li Ssu. Take yin and yang. The ' Western Inscription ' (Hsi-ming) says that the principle is one but its manifestations are many. The meaning is the same here." Chu Hsi also said, "The more things are differentiated, the greater the principle appear." [19]

Chu Hsi takes principle as substance because first there is substance and then there is function. Function is consistent with (in accordance with) principle. But with respect to original substance, what is important is not the relationship of substance and function but the relationship of principle and existence. What does the existence of this thing take as its original substance? The original substance of somethings existence. The reason of somethings existence must be within the nature of that thing. This thing is this thing because of its nature. The existence of something should have its own original substance, because existence is the existence of the original substance. Original substance is the subject of existence. Besides the original substance, the existing subject also contains many accidentals. Chu Hsi said in relation to original substance.

Therefore when we Confucianists speak of the original substance of the nature, it means only the reality of humanity, righteousness, propriety, and wisdom (jen i li chih)...[20] If is not that the original substance contains these, how can they develop from function? There is no point we can grasp the original substance; we can only look for the original substance its function. [21]

---

(19) Chu Tzu yu-lei, 6:3b, p.164.
(20) The Four Virtues and taught in the Book of Mencius, 2A:6 and 6A:6.
(21) Chu Tzu wen-chi, 61:2a-b, third reply in Lin Te-chiu.

In this quotation Chu Hsi takes humanity, righteousness, propriety, and wisdom as the endowment of nature. The meaning of original substance and the meaning of the original substance of the mind that has not yet begun to work are the same. Here the substance means entity.

> Someone asked, "What is the difference between the mind not yet working and its nature?"

> Chu Hsi replied, "Mind contains substance and function. Before the mind begins to work it is substance. When it is working, it is function."(22)

Chu Hsi advocated that the mind consists of its feeling and its nature. The original substance of its nature is the substance of the mind and the principle of humanity, righteousness, propriety, and wisdom. In the same way the original substance of the mind is also the principle of humanity, righteousness, propriety, and wisdom. "When we talk solely about the virtue of the mind, then the mind not yet functioning is substance and the mind already functioning is function. When we talk only of the principle of love, then humanity is the substance and compassion is the function. (23)

When we take principle or the Way as substance, we contrast it to function and not to existence. According to Chu Hsi, that by which a thing exists has to have principle and material force. The original substance of a thing is therefore formed by the fusion of principle and material force. This original substance then is the root of the thing; all other substance and functions are dependent upon this original substance.

Chu Hsi took principle and material force as the original substance of things, equivalent to things in Western cosmology, not being in Western ontology. But form the point of view of Chinese

---

(22) Chu Tzu yu-lei, 5:7b, p.146.
(23) Ibid., 20:17b, p.752.

philosophy, Chu Hsi's thing which consists of principle and material force is what the Book of Changes spoke of as becoming and actus. The two terms in the Book of Changes refer to the myriad things in the universe, which were formed by change. The becoming and actus of the myriad things are not absolute actus. The absolute actus exhibits no change. It has no element of the perpetual renewal of life. The actus of the myriad things in the universe is formed by fusion and the perpetual renewal of the elements. The Book of Changes took the myriad things to be formed by the material force of yin and yang. Within the material force there is naturally the principle of union. Chu Hsi advocated that principle did not contain material force, but was in opposition to it. The metamorphosis of the myriad things has its own principle of becoming and its own material force of becoming. If there is a certain principle, there is a certain material force. Principle and material force unite and form the myriad things. The Book of Changes takes material force to be the original substance of things. Within material force there is principle. Chu Hsi took principle and material force as the substance of things. Principle and material force are two, but they are not separate.

Chu Hsi's theory of metaphysics, therefore, does not use the categories of hsing-erh-shang and hsing-erh-hsia but begins with original substance. Although material force is hsing-erh-hsia, it is still one element in the original substance of things. Therefore it still belongs to the metaphysics. Things in Western epistemology have two elements: forma and materia. Materia belongs to material; therefore it belongs to the universe. Material force in Chinese philosophy does not mean material. Therefore it belongs to the science of hsing-erh-shang.

III. Principle and Material Force

In studying the substance of the myriad things, Chu Hsi was following Ch'eng I's thought, which advocated that the myriad things are composed principle and material force. Principle forms the nature of the thing and material force forms the form of the thing. "Someone asked, Is the nature the material of life? Chu Hsi replied, No, the nature is the principle of life. Material force is the material of life, and already has form and figure." [24]

The things of the universe are called the myriad things, are not necessarily all material, things represent that which actually exists. Everything has principle by which it is formed and also has "existence" which formed each thing. "Existence" is the concrete thing, that is, the reality of the thing. And principles are abstract, abstract principle which forms reality has to have "material". Material is concrete, and therefore it must have form. Material comes from material force. Therefore everything has both principle and material force.

The word hsing (physical form) was originally written as hsing, which means a model. In ancient China people made bricks by first mixing clay, then spreading it evenly, then taking a wooden model and pressing it on the clay to separate it into suqares. After baking in the sun, the square clay turned into square bricks. If we use this word hsing (model) to explain the substance of things, then this hsing (physical form) is quivalent to the forma in Western scholastic philosophy. This forma then is equivalent to Chu Hsi's principle but not to material force. Therefore the hsing in "material force forms the hsing of things" does not mean model but physical form. As the form depends on the material, it is said: "Material force forms the physical form of things." physical form is the characteristic of material force, but principle has no form and moreover can't have force. Therefore, Chu Hsi advocated that principle is hsing-erh-shang and hsing-erh-hsia.

Material force is the material, equivalent to materia in Western scholastic philosophy. This is speaking of it in terms of function and not from the point of view of its original nature. Material force has the function of materia in the substance of things. Materia in original nature is always of a material nature but material force is not. Material force may be material or may be immaterial.

---

(24) Chu Tzu yu-lei, 137:10a, p. 1239.

Things have their own principle to form things. Principle is the nature of the thing. Things have their own material which is material force. "As there is such principle, then there is such material force." (25)

A thing becomes a certain thing because the principle for it exists; if the principle exists, then so does the material force. For example, a particular person became that particular person because there exists principle of the person and then the material force of the person. The "this" of the person is the characteristic of the person and also the principle of the person. Because the particular principle exists, so does the material force. Chu Hsi often said that principle and material force should not be seen as sequential; but in theory, principle must come first. "Some asked, does principle come first and material force follow it?" Chu Hsi replied, "Principle and material force as such are not sequential; but when we are reasoning, principle comes first and material force follow it'." (26)

This means that principle conditions material force. Principle determines material force. There is a little similarity to the forma determing materia in scholastic philosophy. Materia is an undetermined material; having forma added to it, it becomes materia of the things. But in Chu Hsi's philosophy, the relationship of principle and material force is not like this. Chu Hsi advocated that principle is one but its manifestations are many. Originally principle is one, but because of material force it is manifested as many. In this way of speaking, material force determines principle. First there is a unified principle, but then according to the differences of material force, the things formed are different. The differences of things do not come from principle but from material force.

The thought that principle is one but its manifestations are many comes from Ch'eng I, but Chang Tsai already had this kind of thought. Chu Hsi strongly supported it.

---

(25) Chu Tzu yu-lei, 1:1b, p.2.
(26) Ibid.. 1:2b, p.4.

Someone asked. "What are principle and material force?" Chu Hsi replied, "I ch'uan (Ch'eng I) said it well: ' Principle is one but manifestations are many'.[27] If you take all of heaven and earth and myriad things together, there is only one principle. But each person has his own principle." [28]

" ' The Western Inscription', from beginning to end is explaining this concept that principle is one but manifestations are many." [29]

Chu Hsi takes the Great Ultimate as the supreme principle; but it is not the highest principle of the universe, and it is not the origin of the universe. The Great Ultimate is the most relevant principle of everything. Chu Hsi taught that there is only one Great Ultimate in the universe but that everything has its own Great Ultimate. This is the meaning that principle is one but its manifestations are many.

Chu Hsi said, "The Great Ultimate is only the principle of heaven, earth, and the myriad things. Within heaven and earth, there is the Great Ultimate. Within the myriad phenomena, each phenomenon has its own Great Ultimate." [30]

"The Great Ultimate is only the best and most perfect principle; everyone has a Great Ultimate and everything has a Great Ultimate." [31]

How do we explain this seeming contradiction? Fung Yu-lan said.

According to this, in everything besides principle which forms the thing itself, there is the Great Ultimate. That is, the whole principle of everything. [32] As I have written, "This explana-

(27) I-chuan wen-chi, *Collection of literary works by Cheng I*, 5:12b, in the Erh-Cheng chuan-shu.
(28) Chu Tzu yu-lei, 1:1b, p.2.
(29) Ibid., 98:15a, p.4009.
(30) Ibid., 1:1a, p.1.
(31) Ibid., 94:62, p.3765.
(32) Chung-kuo che-hsueh shih, *History of Chinese Philosophy*, Shanghai: Commerical Press, 1934, p.902.

tion is not correct. Chu Hsi does not separate principle and Great Ultimate as two different kinds of principle. There is only one principle. The Great Ultimate represents the supreme principle, that is, the whole principle. One thing cannot contain two principles, or else it can't be one thing but two. The principle of a thing is the whole principle of the principle of Heaven. It is only manifested to a different degree. Chu Hsi made an analogy: There is only one moon but the moons reflected in the rivers, lakes, and streams are different." [33]

But the problem is here. Principle forms the nature of a thing; it is the principle by which a thing gets its physical form. When the principle is the same, then the nature should be the same. When the nature is the same, the thing is the same. Suppose there is only one principle for all myriad things in the universe. Then there is only one nature. if there is only one nature, then there is only one thing. Then the result of Chu Hsi's thought would be similar to the result of Chuang tzu's (c. 369-c. 286 B.C.) "Chi-wu lun" (On the equality of things), that is, the myriad things are the same. Only the surface appearance differs. All of the substance is the same. For example, the nature of human beings is the same. All person are human. Only their quantity and quality differ.

But this is not the conclusion Chu Hsi wanted. He still brought forth the theory that principle is one but its manifestations are many. But if the principle is one, how can it be manifested differently? If we want to explain this, we must analyze and clarify the content of principle.

The traditional thought of Confucianists took the universe as the flux of life and everything possessing life. Life to them was smiply the existence of things. From the point of view of existence, everything is existent, just as everything is being. The existence of the myriad things was formed by the fusion of yin and yang in their operations. The operations of yin and yang never cease. They are continuous and

---

(33) Chu Tzu yu-lei, 94:35b, p.3824; Lokuang, Chung-kuo che-hsueh ssu-hsiang shih:Sung-tai p'ien, *History of Chinese Philosophical Thought: the Sung period,* Taipei: Student Book Co., 1978, p.499.

uncessingly combine to produce the myriad things. We call their operations the perpetual renewal of life. The Book of Changes says, "The perpetual renewal of life is called Changed." [34]

Because every existence is formed from the operation of yin and yang, each existence is a life. The Book of Changes says, "One yin and one yang is called the Way. That which continues it is goodness. That which is formed is the nature." Yin and yang not only revolve unceasingly in the universe; they also revolve unceasingly in the physical body of each thing. The existence of each physical body never ceases motion. It is a kind of existence of on-going movement. Therefore we call it life.

The whole universe is composed of the operations of yin and yang. Yin and Yang have their own principle of operations. This principle is the principle of perpetual renewal of life. It is also the Great Ultimate that comprises the universe. Chu Hsi thought that the universe has a Great Ultimate. In addition, every physical body also has the principle of the operations of yin and yang. This principle also is the principle of perpetual renewal of life. This is also the Great Ultimate in every physical body. The principle of perpetual renewal of life in everything and in the universe is the same. But the principle of perpetual renewal of life of each thing is different. Therefore Chu Hsi said, "Principle is one but its manifestations are many."

Originally the principle of perpetual renewal of life in each thing is the same principle. Then why is it different? It is different because the material force that each physical body possesses is different. Material force is differentiated into purity and turbidness. The degree of purity or turbidness also has countless varieties diversifications. The effect of purity and turbidness consists in concealing or making manifest the principle of perpetual renewal of life. Turbid material force conceals the principle of perpetual renewal of life. Pure material force makes manifest the principle of perpetual renewal of life. The difference in the degree of pruity or turbidness determines the degree to

---

(34) *Book of Changes*, "Appended Remarks," pt.1, Ch. 5.

which the principle of perpetual renewal of life will be concealed or made manifest. The most turbid material force completely conceals the principle of perpetual renewal of life, causing the physical body not to manifest the slightest amount of life. The lower the degree of turbidndess, the lower the degree of concealment of the principle of perpetual renewal of life. Therefore life is more able to be made manifest. Take, for example, plants. On them the degree of turbidness being low, the degree of concealment of the principle of perpetual renewal of life will be low, and this principle will be manifest. The material force of man, on the other hand, is pure, and therefore man's principle of perpetual renewal of life can be manifestes. This is what Chu Hsi meant when he said that things, that is, animals obtained only part of principle, but man obtained the whole of principle.

> Someone asked, "If someone asked if material force which is upright and unobstructed constitutes man and material force which is oblique and obstructed constitutes things, what would you say?"
>
> Chu Hsi replied, "The coming into existence of things must necessarily depend on the coagulation of material force and then have form. That which possesses pure material force is man; that which possesses turbid material force is a thing ...."
>
> Someone else asked, "What do you think of this: Material force has purity and turbidness but their principle is the same?"

Chu Hsi replied, "It is certainly like that. The principle is like a precious jewel. When possessed by a saint or wise man, it is like being placed in clearwater. Its brilliance naturally can be seen. When it is possessed by stupid or unworthy persons, it is like being placed in turbid water. The water must be made clear and the mud and sand removed before its brilliance can be seen." [35]

---

(35) Chu Tzu yu-lei, 17:4a-5b, pp.600-601.

Even though man's material force may be pure, there are still differences in the degree of purity. Therefore Chu Hsi advocated the nature of the quality of material force. The purity or turbidness of material force makes human nature good or evil. Compared to that of man, the material force of things is turbid, and the principle that things possess is oblique and obstructed. The material force of man, on the other hand, is pure; thus the principle that man possesses is upright and unobstructed.

Principle and material force fuse to form the substance of things. Substance possesses the nature of the thing and its form. In his ontology, St. Thomas Aquinas takes forma and materia to form the nature of things. Nature and existentia fuse to form "reality", which is a concrete thing. The structure of substance for Chu Hsi and St. Thomas Aquinas are similar but there are differences. Figure 1 shows those differences.

Figure 1

Chu Hsi's Theory of Substance

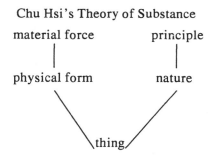

St. Thomas Aquinas' Theory of Substance

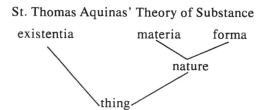

Existentia in St. Thoams Aquinas' theory of substance brings with it the individuality of quantity and quality; besides characteristics in common, the concrete thing has its individuality. Material force in Chu Hsi's theory of substance brings individuality with it, too. Individuality consists of the Five Agents. Chu Hsi calls these Five Agents quality. Quality is formed by material force: "Yang changes and yin fuses with it and thin Water, Fire, Wood, Metal and Earth are produced. Yin and yang are the material force which produces the quality of these Five Agents, when Heaven and Earth produced things, the Five Agents came into existence first." [36]

Chou Tun-i(1017-1073) in his "Explanation of the Diagram of the Great Ultimate" (Tai-chi-t'u shou) advocated that the Ultimate of Nonbeing (wu-chi) begat the Great Ultimate. The Great Ultimate produced yin and yang, which produced the Five Agents. The Five Agents produced male and female. Male and female produced the myriad phenomena. Even though Chu Hsi defended Chou Tun-i's "Explanation of the Diagram of the Great Ultimate," he did not make use of it. He did not advocate that the Great Ultimate produced yin and yang but said that the Great Ultimate was the principle and yin and yang were the material force. The fusion of principle and material force produced things. The fusing of principle and material force produced the Five Agents which are the quality of things. When asked about the theory of the "explanation of the Diagram of the Great Ultimate" Chu Hsi replied, "In speaking of man's physical body, the breath in breathing is the yin and yang, The body, the blood, and the flesh are the Five Agents. Their nature is the principle." [37]

Chu Hsi's theory of substance is as shown in Figure 2. Material force is hsing-shang.

---

(36) Chu Tzu yu-lei, 94:3a, p.3759.
(37) Ibid., 94:11b-12a, pp.376-377.

Figure 2

Chu Hsi's Theory of Substance

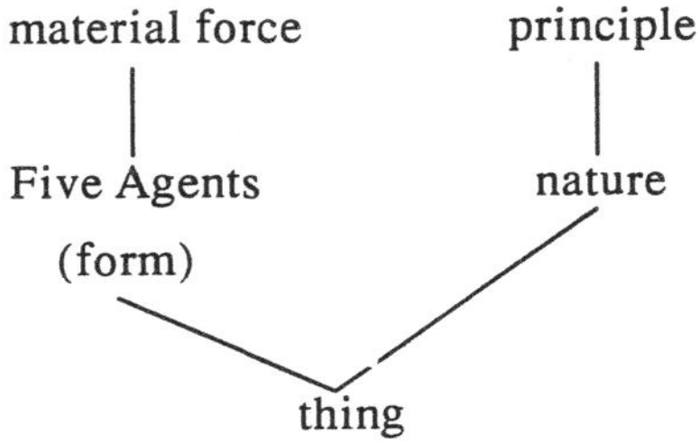

material force   principle

Five Agents   nature

(form)

thing

Chih (material force) and the Five Agents are hsing-hsia. Principle then is hsing-shang. Therefore the substance of things contains hsing-shang and hsing-hsia. As Chu Hsi advocated, there is a distinction between hsing-shang and hsing-hsia, but they cannot be separated.[38] In Chu Hsi's metaphysical structure of the substance, hsing-shang and hsing-hsia are mutually connected.

IV. The Principle of Perpetual Renewal of Life

There is only one principle in Heaven and Earth, yet each thing has a principle. Principle is one but its manifestations are many. This principle is the principle of perpetual renewal of life. What does it involve? Although the principle of perpetual renewal of life which Chu Hsi spoke of is the principle of life, it is different from the principle of life in Western philosophy in general. Although life as spoken of in Western philosophy has various different explanations, the most common explanation is that life is autonomous. Life grows by itself. Chu Hsi spoke of life in the unswerving Confucian traditions life of the mind. Mencius (372-289 B.C.) said that man has smaller parts and greater parts. The smaller parts are the organs like ears and eyes. The greater part is the organ of the mind and tought. [39]   The difference

---

(38) See above, n.9

(39) Book of Mencius, 6A:14-15.

between man and animals is in this greater part. Mencius said, "The difference between the superior man and the common people is that he preserves and fosters his mind." [40]

The human mind is unobstructed and flexible; it can know and think and make determinations. It commands nature and feeling. Therefore the mind contains the whole principle of perpetual renewal of life. As Chu Hsi noted, "The whole of the mind is clear and open; it contains myriad principles." [41] "The mind is the myriad principles; only the one who can preserve the mind can probe to the root of the principle." [42] "Nature is the principle which the mind possesses, and the mind is the place where the principles converge." [43]

Chu Hsi takes the mind as commanding the nature of thing and its feeling. The nature is the substance of the mind; feeling is the usage of the mind. The principle of the nature composses humanity, righteousness, propriety, and wisdom. The usage of the mind comprises the feeling of commiseration, shame, right and wrong, and humility.

> Someone asked about mind, nature and feeling. Chu Hsi replied, "Mencius said the feeling of commiseration of the mind is the beginning of humanity. From this one section all becomes clear. The feeling of commiseration, shame, right and wrong, and humility are all feelings. Humanity, righteousness, propriety, and wisdom are the substance of the nature. Within the nature there are only humanity, righteousness, propriety, and wisdom. It is expressed as the feeling of commiseration, shame, humility, right and wrong. Therefore it is the feeling of the nature." [44]

This section make it clear that the principle contained in the human mind is the nature. The nature is then humanity, righteousness,

---

(40) Book of Mencius, 4A:28.
(41) Chu Tzu yu-lei, 5:11a, p.153.
(42) Ibid., 9:6a, p.245.
(43) Ibid., 5:6a, p.143.
(44) Ibid., 5:6b, p.148.

propriety, and wisdom. The principle of perpetual renewal of life for Chu Hsi is humanity, righteousness, propriety, and wisdom. These four qualities generalized are humanity. Mencius said, "humanity is the human mind." [45] He also said, "As for humanity, it is man; combining the two forms the Way." [46] Chu Hsi explains the mind of man being humanity as man possessing the mind of Heaven and Earth as his mind. Heaven and Earth take the creation of things as their mind. The mind of man therefore is humanity. Humanity is creation (sheng). To clarify the meaning of the word "mind", Chu Hsi said.

> One word can cover it all. That is simply creation. The great virtue of Heaven and Earth is creation. Man receives the element of Heaven and Earth is created. Therefore this mind must be human. Humanity is then creation. [47]

> Heaven and Earth take creation of things as their mind. And the creation of man and things likewise take the mind of Heaven and Earth as their mind. Therefore we say that although the virtue of the mind encompasses all and there is nothing which it does not contain, one word can cover it all. Thus I say simple humanity. [48]

The principle possessed by Heaven and Earth (the Great Ultimate of Heaven and Earth) is the principle that produces and reproduces the myriad things. It is called the mind of Heaven and Earth, that is, the principle of perpetual renewal of life of Heaven and Earth.

Man possesses the material force of yin and yang, of Heaven and Earth, and thus possesses the principle of perpetual renewal of life. Man's principle of perpetual renewal of life is called humanity. The myriad things all possess the principle of perpetual renewal of life of Heaven and Earth: "The mind of Heaven which produces things never ceases .... The Way of ch'ien (Heaven) [49] changes and perpetually

---

(45) *Book of Mencius*, 6A:11.
(46) Ibid., 7B:16.
(47) Chu Tzu yu-lei, 5:3b, p.138.
(48) Chu Tzy wen-chi, 67:20a, "*A Treatise on Humanity.*"
(49) The first hexagram in the *Book of Chanegs.*

renews life. Each thing obtains its proper nature and life. Therefore it makes each grass and tree obtain its principle." [50]

But the myriad things do not have the faculty of mind and tought. They cannot recognize the principle of perpetual renewal of life and cannot experience it, much less manifest and develop it. Man has the faculty of mind and thought. Man has feeling; he knows to love his own life and the life of other men and things. Chu Hsi takes humanity as the principle of love: "Love is not humanity; the principle of love is humanity. The mind is not humanity; its virtue is humanity."[51]

Humanity is the principle of love. This kind of love is not lust for things but for virtue. The mind of man puts into practice the virtue of humanity and love. Therefore man has the feeling of commiseration, shame and dislike, right and wrong, and humility. Chu Hsi takes feeling as emanating from the nature; that is, emanating from the principle of the mind. Commiseration, shame and dislike, right and worng, and humility are feelings. Thus the minds action is the beginning of virtue. Mencius said, "The feeling of commiseration of the mind is the beginning of humanity. The feeling of shame and dislike of the mind is the beginning of propriety. The feeling of humility of the mind is the beginning of prporiety. The feeling of right and wrong of the mind is the beginning of wisdom. Man has these four beginnings just as he has four limbs." [52]

The nature possessed by man's substance is the principle of humanity, righteousness, propriety, and wisdom. The material force possessed by man's substance is the feeling of commiseration, shame and dislike, right and wrong, and humility. The substance of man is the goodness of ethical morality. Man according to his substance is moral. The principle of perpetual renewal of life is the principle of humanity, righteousness, propriety, and wisdom. What is called perpetual renewal of life is spiritual life, is the activity of the mind and spirit.

---

(50) Chu Tzu yu-lei, 27:28b, p.1108.
(51) Ibid., 20:24A, p.765.
(52) *Book of Mencius*, 2A:6.

Heaven and earth and all the myriad things of the universe possess this kind of principle. The degree of manifestation of the principle of spiritual life is different depending on whether the material force that forms it is either pure or turbid. The material force of man is pure, and thus his spiritual life can be manifested. Therefore it is said that the principle man possesses is complete, upright, and unobstructed. However, within the material force of man there are differences of degree of purity. A lower degree of purity in the material force produces turbid material force. Man who possess this kind of material force are evil. The material force possessed by sages is the purest. The spiritual life of sages is thus completely manifested. The "Appended Remarks" of the Book of Changes says, "The great virtue of Heaven and Earth is creation. The great preciousness of saints is called rank. How to preserve this rank is called humanity." [53]

The virtue of the humanity of sages matches the virtue of creation of Heaven and Earth. Thus the Book of Changes says, "As for the great man, his virtue matches that of Heaven and Earth, his brightness matches that of the sun and moon, his orderliness matches that of the four seasons, and his auspiciousness and inauspiciousness matches that of ghosts and spirits." [54] Chu Hsi said.

The universe is only the flowing of one material force. The myriad things are naturally produced and naturally grow and form and have their own color. Are they one by one decorated this? A sage is only a flowing out from the great origin. His vision is naturally clear. His hearing is naturally sharp. His disposition is naturally gentle. His appearance is naturally respectful. The relation of father and son is therefore humane. The relationship of ruler and minister is therefore righteousness. The many principles flowing out of the great origin are only this one from beginning to end. [55]

---

(53) *Book of Changes*, "Appended Remarks," pt.2, Ch. 10.
(54) *Book of Changes*, the main commentary on the first hexagram, ch'ien.
(55) Chu Tzu yu-lei, 45:2A-b, pp.1825-1826.

The sage represents the whole meaning of the principle of perpetual renewal of life. He is also the whole expression of that principle. Sages and Heaven and Earth match each other. Heaven and Earth are characterized by creation, and sages are characterized by humanity. Creation and humanity match each other.

V. The Metaphysical Basis of Morality

Morality is the expression of spiritual life. When Chu Hsi spoke of morality he often talked about the Five Constant virtues of humanity, righteousness, propriety, wisdom, and faithfulness. The Five Constant Virtues are man's spiritual life. In his theory of substance, Chu Hsi took principle and material force to be the metaphysical structure. Principle becomes the nature; material force becomes concrete form. The form of material force first has yin and yang, then the Five Agents. Afterwards comes the individuality of things. In the universe yin and yang become the Five Agents, which operate as Origination, Flourish Advantage, and Firmness (yuan heng li chen) [56]. Within humans, yin and yang become the Five Agents, which correspond to humanity, righteousness, propriety, wisdom, and faithfulness.

> Origination, Flourish Advantage, and Firmness are the nature; bright, growth, harvest, and storage are feelings. As for the mind, it takes Origination to create; it takes Flourish to grow; it takes Advantage to harvest; and it takes Firmness to store. As for the nature, it is humanity, righteousness, propriety, wisdom, and faithfulness. As for feeling, it is commiseration, shame and dislike, humility, and right and wrong. As for the mind, it takes humanity to love, it takes righteousness to dislike, it takes propriety to be humble, and it takes wisdom to be wise. As for the nature, it is the principle of the mind. As for feeling, it is the function of the mind. [57]

---

(56) The Four Qualities of the first hexagram, ch'ien, in the *Book of Changes*.

(57) Chu Tzu wen-chi, 67:1a, *A Treatise on Origination, Flourish, Advantage, and Firmness.*

Humanity, righteousness, propriety, wisdom, and faithfulness match Wood, Fire, Metal, Water, and Earth. Earth is the basis of Wood, Fire, Metal, and Water. When the Five Agents match the five directions, the Earth matches the center; when the Five Agents match the four seasons, Earth is the central point of the year. When the Five Agents match the Five constant Virtues, Earth matches faithfulness. Faithfulness is the common condition of humanity, righteousness, propriety, and wisdom, that is, sincerity in nature. Thus, the usage of the Five Constant Virtues only has the Four Virtues of humanity, righteousness, propriety, and wisdom. The Four Virtues then match Origination, Flourish, Advantage, and Firmness.

The great virtue of Heaven and Earth is called creation, Heaven and Earth produce the myriad things through a process of birth, growth, harvest, and storage. Origination is the birth, Flourish is the growth, Advantage is the harvest, and Firmness is the storage. The external form of Originatoin, Flourish, Advantage, and Firmness is the four seasons of spring, summer, autumn, and winter. Therefore it is said that in the spring there is birth, in the summer there is growth, in the autumn there is harvest, and in the winter there is storage. Man's spiritual life also has its own process, which is humanity, righteousness, propriety, and wisdom.

Ethical morality is not only ethical behavior and the habit of humanity. Western ethics takes goodness as the habit of being good fostered by charitable action. It has no relationship to the theory of substance. Good or evil in man does not influence his basic nature. Men who do evil actions do not decrease their substance. Good men are men; evil men are also men. In Chinese philosophy, such as in Chu Hsi's philosophy, morality is not only humane action, but it is also the expression of a man's substance. In the Doctrine of the Mean it is called full development of one's substance. In the Doctrine of the Mean is human nature. The Doctrine of the Mean says, "Only people of the utmost sincerity under Heaven can develop fully their nature; developing fully this nature can thus develop fully the nature of others;

developing fully the nature of others thus can develop fully the nature of things." Chu Hsi said. [58]

> By utmost sincerity in the universe is meant the reality of the virtue of the sage. The universe cannot add to it. As one who fully develops his nature, his virtue is solid. Because he possesses no selfish human desires and because the Mandate of Heaven is within him, he can be aware of it, follow it whether it be great or small, coarse or refined. There is not even the slightest bit that will not be developed. The nature of man and things is also my nature; but since they are endowed with different material force and physical forms, so there are differences. He who can fully develop is said to know with clarity and to handle without impropriety. [59]

The nature of man is humanity. Fully developing one's nature then is to develop humanity and love, to love one's own life, to love the life of others, and to love the life of the myriad things. The Doctrine of the Mean says, "He who can develop the nature of things can then assist Heaven and Earth in renewing and fostering. He who can assist Heaven and Earth in renewing and fostering can then be in the same rank of Heaven and Earth."[60] Developing humanity and love is to assist Heaven and Earth in the perpetual renewal of the myriad things. Man thus can be in the same rank as Heaven and Earth. In the "Appended Remarks" we read, "As for the great man, his virtue matches with Heaven and Earth." [61]

Ethical morality is connected to the metaphysical substance. Ethical morality takes substance as its basis. Western ethics takes morality

---

(58) *Doctrine of the Mean*, Ch. 22.

(59) Chung-yung chang-chu, Commentary on the Doctrine of the Mean, Comment on Ch. 22.

(60) *Doctrine of the Mean*, Ch. 22.

(61) *Book of Changes*, the main commentary on the first hexagram, Ch'ien.

as rooted in human nature, for in human nature there are rules of morality. The ethics of Chu Hsi and the Confucianist take morality to originate in the substance of man; morality is the development of human life, because the principle of humanity, righteousness, propriety, and wisdom is the principle of perpetual renewal of life. The principle of perpetual renewal of life is the principle of the substance of man.

The principle of man and things is the same. The nature of man and things is also my nature, but since they are endowed with different material force and physical forms, so there are differences. The myriad phenomena in the universe all have the principle of humanity. It is only because of the turbidness of their material force that it cannot be made manifest. The material force of man is pure. Thus it can manifest the principle of humanity.

VI. Conclusion

Chu Hsi's theory of metaphysical structure concerns the substance of things. The substance of things was formed by principle and material force. Principle became the nature of the thing and material force became the form of the thing. The nature of the thing is the principle of why a particular thing is itself. The form is the material of why it became itself. Material comes from material force. Material force first forms the Five Agents, and then from the Five Agents it forms the material.

The principle of things is one principle. Chu Hsi advocated that principle one but its manifestation are many. The principle of things is the principle of actual "existence."

The existence of things is formed by the union of principle of yin and yang. The union of yin and yang then is the continuous operation of "becoming". The operations of yin and yang, which never cease, produce the myriad things. The principle of the union of yin and yang is the principle of perpetual renewal of life.

The principle of perpetual renewal of life in the myriad things of the universe, in each of phenomenons, is the same principle. Yet because the material force endowed by each is different, the principle manifested in the myriad things appears to be different. Material force can be pure or turbid. Turbid material force conceals the principle of perpetual renewal of life. Pure material force manifests the principle of perpetual renewal of life. The material force of things turbid. The material force of man is pure.

The principle of perpetual renewal of life manifested in man is humanity, righteousness, propriety, and wisdom in spiritual life; generalized, these become humanity. Man's principle of perpetual of life then is humanity.

The principle of Heaven and Earth is perpetual renewal of life. The principle of man is humanity. From creation there is humanity. In the myriad things of the universe there is creation, and in man there is humanity. Perpetual renewal of life in Heaven and Earth passes through four processes which are Origination, Flourish, Advantage, and Firmness. The spiritual life of man so passes through four processes, which are humanity, righteousness, propriety, and wisdom. These belong to the substance of man and the characteristics of the substance. Thus ethical morality and the characteristics of the substance connect with each other. Chu Hsi's theory of metaphysical structure combined substance and morality, and connected ethics and ontology. Thus, although the philosophy of Chinese Confucianism seems to have only ethics, actually its ethics are the continuation of ontology. Its ethics and ontology are mutually connected.

Persona: Its Potential Significance in Contemporary Philosophy

I. Western Philosophy

Originating from the Greeks, western philosophy searches for the truth in its attempts to study the meaning of things in the universe. Things in the universe are individual and distinct from one another. Studying each one individually is not possible owing to constraints in time and manpower. Even if we were to contribute our time and effort to study them, results would still be individual and unique, and therefore, wanting in scholastic significance. For these individual and unique studies to be of scholastic value, they must lead to common, universally applicable concepts and principles. Throught these concepts and principles, things are bound together to form systems. From this, we see why western philosophy tends towards common concepts and principles.

The most basic concepts and principles applicable to the universe include those of "being", "existence" and "nature" which together form the structure of western metaphysical ontology. The most basic principle are the laws of indentity, non-contradicition, and causality all of which are also fundamental to ontology.

These concepts dominated ontological studies from the time of the Greek philosophy to the European philosophy of the Middle Ages. Although Greek philosophy also included the concept of "substance" (substantia), its discussion was limited to the abstract aspect. The Greek came up with hypostasis, or the Latin suppositum, meaning "individual being". When referring to an individual being of a human nature, the term "persona" is used. The latter term was likewise only taken as a concept and not reckoned as a subject of study.

In Catholicism, which reached Europe and later became the Europeans' common faith, the dogma of the Blessed Trinity is one basic tenet. To express this faith, Catholic theologians borrowed philosophical concepts to express that there are three persons in one God.

Thus, the concept of person became an important part of Catholic theology. Furthermore, theologians used scholastic philosophical ideas to go deeper in the study of the concept of person.

Theologians share one common consensus on this concept, i.e., "person" has a complex meaning that includes the essentia individuata, subsistentia and accidentia.

Theologians are divided on the origin of this concept. Cardianl Petrus Parente, who was my dogmatic theology professor at the Propaganda University in Rome, designed the following diagram in his book on the Holy Trinity (De Deo Trino) [1]:

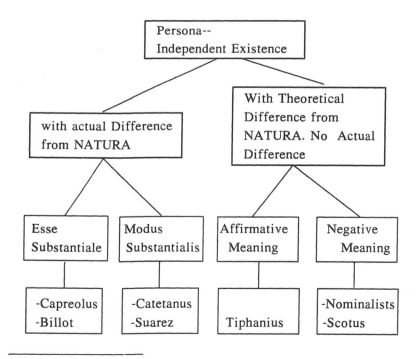

(1) Petrus Parents, De Deo Trino, P.85, Rome 1983.

God has a unique onological nature. The terms unique and single differ in meaning, the former being positive while the latter being negative. A unique ontological nature possesses every perfection and does not require any relationship with matters outside itself. On the other hand, single connotes the same lack of external relationship but at the same time, may need such relationships by nature. God is unique and does not have any relationship whatsoever except internally. Because God is absolute, the ideas of posse and becoming do not apply to Him. He is totally a unity of being and functions. Thus, relationship within the being is one of ontological unity. God's ontological relationship is divided into two absolute beings that constitute two persons. This explains why God is Trinity. Since the being of these Three persons is one, therefore, God is three persons with one nature.

I do not intend to discuss theology here. I only wish to point out that Catholic theologians use the concept of subsistance to explain "person", although actual explanations very from school to school.

No Special interest was given to "person" in western philosophy from the Middle Ages to present times, whether in Scholastic philosophy or in other schools. However, contemporary Philosophy started to give attention to the independent individual. Bergson talked about the fluidity of life. The Existentialists proposed the idea of concrete existence while Whitehead talked about concrete events. Existentialism likened concrete existence with man's existence, after which it proceeded to the discussion of the "ego". In Italy, there was the so-called human logic or Ermeneutica umana, which is nothing but personalism. It studies the concept. All common characteristics of man, such as sex, age, traits, qualities, etc. acquire differences and variations when analyzed and explained using this concept. Therefore, the concept of person is basis to the study of man. When used to explain human nature, it denies a common nature. Instead, it only recognizes the nature (characteristics) of each individual. This is quite similar to the qualitative nature proposed by Chu Hsi.[2] In contemporary Euro-

---

(2) Laura Paoleti, *Ermeneutica delle condizioni umane*, Edizioni fondazione, Nova Spes, Rome, 1990, p.151.

pean and American societies, everyone stresses on his own persona. This is especially true among the youth who are well aware of its importance.

II. Chinese Philosophy

Chinese philosophy tends to stress the actual individual. The Chinese system of writing is basically related to shape and sound. We also know that both the senses of sight and hearing have their targets in actual objects or individuals. Because of this, the Chinese writing system developed in such a way that it is lacking in terms to express abstract concepts. Judging from the Chinese way of writing, we can conclude that the Chinese often base their reasoning on concrete events or views of ancestors and seldom think using abstract lines of thought.[3] From these, we can conclude that Chinese philosophy is pragmatic as differentiated from the abstract Indian philosophy. This pragmatic philosophy deals with the way of human life, centering on man, and thus, is considered a humanist philosophy. Humanism, centered on the actual man, gives importance to each individual person. Confucius' teachings revolved around the virtue of "benevolence". Yet when asked by students to explain benevolence, Confucius responded according to the student's individual qualities. Hence, all his answers varied. This was because he taught based on each student's personal situation. Confucius' moral yardstick is the li (rites). For him, li consists in assigning different positions to different persons. Thus, he stressed on clearly marking out the roles of each one: emperor, official, father, son, husband, wife....to which specific rights and duties correspond. Disputes on the Confucian views on man's inherent good or evil nature went on for more than a thousand years. Chu Hsi, a scholar who searched for a final answer on this issue came up with a conclusion: Good or evil nature can not be determined

---

(3) Hajime Nakamura, Modes of Thought of East Asian People, Chinese translation by Lin T'ai, Ma Hsiao-he, Suhsin Publications.
Chatper entitled "Chinese Modes of Thought", translated by Hsu Fu-kian, Student Book Store Publications.

by using the abstract idea of cosmic nature. Instead, it must be determined by each actual person's dividual qualities. Good or evil nature rests on the individual itself.

Although the word "persona" does not have an equivalent in traditional Chinese philosophy (nor anything closely resembling this word) , its significance was always there. In fact, it received much importance, it being the subject of humanist philosophy. Confucian humanism starts with the concepts of principles (li), material force (ch'i), yin and yang, to arrive at man. To discuss man, Confucianism uses human nature which is rooted in the human heart. For instance, Chu Hsi proposed that one's emotions and qualities can be controlled using the heart. Wang Yang-ming believed that Lu Hsiang-shan adopted Mencius ideas on the heart. Lu later proposed self-evaluation as a means to distinguish good from evil. Wang himself continuned from Lu Hsiang-shan by proposing the idea of conscience, which he defined as the yardstick of every individual's actual behavior. Wang's idea of "unity between consciousness and behavior" is itself based on "persona".

The Confucian idea of cultivating one's moral character is likewise based on "persona". The main topics of the Tah-sueh (Great Learning) are thus centered on the upward ad downward relationship involving the "self", with the cultivation of the individual positioned at the middle, i.e:

> "....those who wished to shine with the illustrious power of personality throughout the Great Society, first hand to govern their nations efficiently. Wishing to do this, they first had to make an ordered harmony in their own families. Wishing to do this, they first had to cultivate their individual selves. Wishing to do this, they first had to put their minds right. Wishing to do this, they first had to make their purposes genuine. Wishing to do this, they first had to extend their knowledge to the utmost. Such extension of knowledge consists in appreciating the nature of things."

Hence, the Chungyung talks about proper solitary behavior (shentu) and sincerity. Chu Hsi dealt with self-admonition while Wang yang-ming stressed conscience. All these ways of cultivating moral character often consist in controlling one's passion to alter personal qualities and form one's spirit. From these, we see that although Chinese traditional philosophy did not have a corresponding term for "persona", its significance did exist. Certainly, it is not the way Hajime Nakamura described as individualistic, selfish "hopes that the sages benefit from it but without wishing them to educate the people."[4] Confucianism proposed that the sage prasies the creation of the cosmos to benefit the people who learn to exercise benevolence. Hence, nothing exists outside the scope of a benevolent heart. As Chang Tsai once proposed in his effort to stress benevolent: "nothing exists beyond the heart." Speaking on the principles of heaven, Lu Hsiang-shan proposed that principles do not hold beyond the heart. Regarding human life, Wang Yang-ming taught the concept of a universal benevolence. These ideas are somewhat similar to western theological concepts. Chinese philosophy takes man as the representative of the whole cosmos. Since each man is a "person", the man's persona encompasses the whole cosmos. In fact, man is the universe itself. As such, man's life and the life of the whole cosmos are one.

III. Philosophy of Life and the Persona

Philosophy of life talks about being from the idea of existence. The being discussed is a concrete, or an actual being. In talking about man, it refers to an actual an concrete being, i.e. a person.

The concept of persona comes after the idea of existence. Since existence requires life, then persona is also derived from life.

A single person is one persona. That comes as a result of his life. Without life, neither he nor his persona would exist.

Persona represents one whole person, indivisible because of his life. Human existence consists in a life of spiritual and bodily unity.

---

(4) Ibid., p.224.

Therefore, man's persona is one that is also a union of spirit and body, or what is ordinarily known as personality. After death, the soul continues to live in a life that is solely spiritual, and therefore, not to be considered a whole person. It always tends toward union with a body.

The life of a unified spirit and body has a physical life. It is manifested physically and is a persona by itself. Women aspire for a beautiful personality. They even include their clothes in their persona, never permitting others to copy their attire. The life of a unified body and spirit also includes emotions and feelings or what is known as one's personality. It is also manifested morally as one's moral character. Personality and moral character are nothing but the individual's persona or individualness. The life of a unified spirit and body possesses rationality as manifested in mental thought or artistic inclination. A person's thoughts, scholastic ideas, and literary artistic works represent him. They contribute to the formation of his own personality or persona.

Man's life is not solitary. He socializes with others and forms relationships with them. These relationships create rights and duties which the ancients called minghen (personal status). Thus, personal stauts also forms one's personality or persona which one keeps safe from the harm of others. A non-human entity invested with legal duties and rights is called "legal person". This is a persona, legally speaking.

Any persona is based on human life. Life is itself persona.

Contemporary western philosophy tends to emphasize "ego". From an abstract concept, it leads to the actual subjcet, and finally gives birth to actual philosophical thought. These philosophies include Existentialism, Structuralism, Semantic Logic, Ermeneutica Umana and the thoughts of Bergson and Whitehead.

Chinese philosophy traditionally emphasizes the importance of actual human life. It often aims at the "persona" as the target of the cultivation of one's moral character.

An actual person is a living person, a life in itself. Thus, we talk about philosophy of life. The life of the universe is inseparable from man's life. Human life encompasses the life of the cosmos which it symbolizes. Human life is a persona, its source is the creative power of the cosmos which is derived from the Creator's creative power. God's creative power is attributed to the Third Person of Blessed Trinity--the Holy Spirit. The Catholic Faith professes that the Divine Word created the universe. Hence, we can say that God's persona is the creator of the human persona.

The Basis of Unum

I. The Unum of Concrete Realities

In philosophy, ordinary concepts in human society often become profound issues. *Being* is one word often said many times in daily life, even by children. In philosophy however, *being* becomes the focus of metaphysical studies, a topic of the highest philosophical level. Similarly, *one* is also a word used in everyday language. But in philosophy, the same word constitutes a problem of the deepest nature in metaphysics. It is an issue debated upon by philosophers who hardly reach a conclusion on its meaning.

I would like to discuss three issues about *one* (Unum). First, how can an actual being become one? Second, since actual beings are constantly in the process of change, what makes them constantly one? The third is a problem related to *persona*. What are the basic constituents of a *persona*? All theses questions are mutually related.

What makes an actual being one?

What makes a table one table and not many? Why is it that an unum must have its components together? Why is a person one person? and a tree one tree?

The reason why a table is a table is that the plan combined the different parts into one table. A house is a house because the construction plan joined all parts together to form a house. This is evident to all. Materials are needed to create a table or a house. In addition, a construction plan is likewise needed. The material is corporeal matter (*chih*) and the plan is the principle (*li*) or the shape. Matter can be comparable to *ch'i* (material force) and from comparable to *li*. Things are made up of material and form, or of *li* and *chi*. A table or a house is one because of its shape. A thing is one because of its form or *li*.

Speaking in an abstract, theoretical manner, a plan for a house or a table joins different parts into something in the shape of a house or table. In practical terms, however, the plan can only delineate the position of each component. It cannot make all parts form one single table or house. In my dicsussion of concrete realities, I have already said that *chih* and *li* together form "nature". Nature and existence together form a concrete begin. Theoretically, it is possible to say that nature and existence form the *substance*. In practical terms, existence requires a creative power to be able to unite with nature so as to form an actual begin. Therefore, the cause of an actual reality is mainly existence. Existence itself is power -- creative power. Creative power is life itself.

Man is a rational animal. A rational animal is "existing" if this person exists. This person exists because he lives. If he's not living, then he doesn't exist at all. Immediately after death, a person may appear like any rational animal, but he no longer is a man because he's dead and no longer rational. Therefore, man's existence is life itself. Of course, one may say that rationality is man's form or man's formal *li*. The form of man is the soul. Hence, the soul is the reason why man "exists", and not because of the life of the creative power. If rationality as the form of man is but an abstract one, then it must not be able to cause man's "existence". If the soul is man's formal *li*, then the soul should not be abstract, but must be the soul that causes actual existence or human life itself. Once the soul leaves, man loses life and no longer exists. Man's existence is life itself and life is man's soul. Man exists through the soul and through soul man becomes one. Soul is itself man's creative power.

The soul makes man's every component to unit and form one person. It unites and ecompasses each component. Every part of man has life. A limb or a finger that loses its function has no life and therefore separates from the body.

A tree or a flowering plant becomes one because of its life. A trunk of a tree or a leaf of a flowering plant unites to become one because of the life of the tree or plant. A things exists because of its life. If a branch or a leaf dries up and loses life, it separated from the one body. If the tree or the plant itself dries up and dies, its branches and leaves also separate and die. The life of the tree or of the plants is itself the creative power of the said tree or plant.

A piece of stone or a mountain is made up of many components bound together by an inner force. This force also causes inner changes to happen within this piece of stone or this mountain. Although this force does not compare with those of animals or plants where it goes around, it likewise reaches every component part of the whole. If not, that component would be detached from the whole. The ancient Chinese often say that each mountain has its own veins. Improper cultivation of mountains destroys these veins to cause avalanches. Inanimate objects also possess an immanent creative power. From this, we see that Chinese philosophy recognizes the existence of life.

Every concrete reality is a subsistent because of its existence. Existence is an active presence. It is life or creative power itself.

II. The Identify of Concrete Realities comes from Creative Power

In philosophy, two questions arise from the concept of one concrete reality. Ths first is related with how the same type of objects become a multiple. For instance, in a multiple of persons, what makes a person one? The second is related with identify. What makes one person the same one from his birth to old age?

Scholastic philosophy explains the concept of "individual" through the concept of matter. The same type of things share the same form. What makes an individual is matter's function of being quantifiable in an actual object. Examples include how high a person's intelligent quotient is or persons' body weight and height, skin color, and the relative positions of one's eyes, ears, nose and mouth. All these characteristics are derived from matter. That is, matter limits the quantity of form which in turn affects the number of individuals. Chu Hsi, a Chinese philosopher, proposed that the individual is derived from *ch'i* (material force). *Li* is the material principle while *ch'i* is the material form. Individuals differ not because of the material principle but because of material form. In turn, material form depends on the purity or turbidity of the *ch'i* (material force).

From where does the quantity or purity of an individual arise? That is to say, how come my intelligence is this much and how come my external appearance is like this? Chinese philosophy says that it is life. Mencius himself talked about nature and life. A person's human nature is determined by the Mandate of Heaven (*t'ien-ming*). A person's characteristics, or what Chu Hsi called qualitative nature, are also determined by the Mandate of Heaven because *chi'* cannot determine a person's clarity. Human *chi'* is much purer than those of material objects. That is because man has a human nature. Differences in the clarity of persons' *ch'i* are determined by the Mandate of Heaven. Although matter or *ch'i* limits physical form (or *li*) and it forms human nature into personal characteristics, what determines the quantity of matter or the clarity and turbidity of *ch'i* is not chance as proposed by Chu Hsi.

In his *Classified Conversations* (*Chu Tzu yulei*), Chu Hsi said: "Those endowed with refined and brilliant material force will become sages and men of virtue, and will be enabled to acquire a comprehensive and correct principle. Those endowed with clear and bright material force will become talented and forthright. Those endowed with simple and rich material force will become mild. Those endowed with pure and lofty material force will become noble. Those endowed with full and thick material force will become rich. Those endowed with long lasting material force will live long. Those endowed with thin and turbid material force will become foolish, unworth, poor, humble, and short-lived.

He said moreover: "Although nature is the same in all men, it is inevitable that in most cases the various elements in their material endowment are unbalanced." (*Chu Tzu yulei*, Book 1, The Nature of Things and Men, Qualitative Nature)

Someone asked him: "There's *yin* and *yang*. They are supposed to be balanced. But why is that the wise and the unwise do not come in the right proportion? Why is it that gentlemen are few and bad men all too many?" He answered: "That's because it's such a complicated matter. How do you expect them to come in a balanced proportion?"

Again, someone asked: "As such, are sages then born by chance and not by a will of heaven? He anwered: "Heaven and earth never said that it will deliberately cause a sage to be born in someplace. Sages are born where *ch'i* goes by chance." (*Chu Tzu yulei*, Book 1, The Nature of Things and Men, Qualitative Nature)

Since *ch'i* and quantity are determined by the Madate of Heaven, we cannot say that the Mandate is influenced by chance. The Mandate of Heaven is not derived from nature but is the will of heaven. Nature is but just a tool of heaven. In Scholastic Philosophy, this is referred to by St. Thomas as God, the Providence who created the universe and the ruler of everything in the universe. This providence is also called continued creation. God created everything in the universe with His creative power. This creative power causes other creative powers. Thus, this creative power continuously causes change in the universe in its act of creation. The Mandate of Heaven is exactly this creative activity of providing the nature and characteristics of things through the action of creative power. Therefore, by the action of creative power, nature and characteristics come from the Mandate of Heaven derived from the Creator. As such, formally speaking, what makes an individual an individual is matter or *ch'i*, or in actual terms, creative power.

Both Confucius and Mencius agreed that life has human nature and characteristics. They in fact accepted fate in life. Mencius once said: The fact that I did not meet the Duke of Lu is because of fate. The son of Chang has no power over why I did not meet the Duke." (*Lianghuiwang*) Human life continues to go on, always experiencing events whether big or small. All of these are affected by human affairs and nature environment. As the Creator holds the myriads of things in the universe, he allows man and nature environment to proceed unimpeded. However, for some events that are important for one person, the human society or a nation, the Creator acts with his providence. This providence is likewise carried out through creative power. Supernaturally, providence of God is directly carried out by the Holy Spirit.

Concrete realities are individuals continuously undergoing change while remaining the same realities. For human beings, this is referred to as ego. From youth to old age, a person is one ego. No matter how the body, intelligence or character change, an ego remains to be itself. How exactly is the "ego" created?

We all know that ego must not be viewed in terms of the collective because our bodies often change. Neither can ego be viewed in terms of the spirit as its functions such as intelligence and character always undergo change. Some philosophers suggested that memory makes one recall who he was before.

This explanation does not hold water. A person who loses his memory remains the same person. Even a person who retained his memory but does not use it reamins the same person as before. Still other philosophers claimed it is self-awareness since each person is aware that he is the same person as always. This too does not hold true as it persents the same problem as memory, or even more. Not only do I know that I am the same person as before, I also know others are the same persons as before. A dog, flower or stone remain the same dog, flower or stone. Anything existing retains its body as before. This is also true with spiritual beings. An angel remains the same angle as before. The Creator remains the same Creator as before. Thus, it is evident that identity can not be explained spiritually but through substance.

Scholastic philosophy explains the concept of identity using the idea of substance. The substance of a concrete reality remains constant although its accidents may change. The reason why I remain I is that my substance remains the same. Only my accidents change. When I explain the concept of concrete realities, I always say that these realities are complete. Completeness of the one depends upon creative power, or existence or life. Substance is an abstract concept like "nature" and "existence". The abstract substance becomes a concrete reality through the action of creative power. Actual concrete realities often change also because of creative power. Although creative power is constantly moving, it remains the same creative power in a concrete reality whose nature it bestows. The creative power of a concrete reality is nothing but the existence of this concrete reality. The creative power of a concrete reality always remains the same reality.

What makes "me" always remain the same "me" is my existence or my life. Life makes me become a concrete being that is unique and that constitutes an individual "me". As long as this concrete being exists, it remains is. "Me" is an integral "me", a concrete being and not an abstract one. The integral me is me owing to my life that remains tha same. Once I cease living, I also cease being me. A flower or a dog remains the same flower or dog because each has the same life or creative power all along. Similarly, a rock, a table or a pen always remains the same rock, table or pen not because they don't change but because of their innate creative power. This creative power makes them one and capable of inner changes, thus making them moving subsistents. As long as their innate creative power remain the same, they always remain the same one being.

Simply stated, the scholastic philosophical principle of indentity is based on nature, an abstract reality. The "identity" I propose is based on creative power which is both a concrete reality and an integral actual reality. Scholastic philosophy explains the concept of being in an abstract manner while I used the traditonal Chinese philosophical concept of substance.

III. Persona

In modern day language, the word identity refers to a person's "role" in society. Confucius himself stressed personal identity. Thus, father, son, emperor, official, etc. each represents a type of identity to which specific rights and duties are attached. These names are abstract. In Chinese opera, concrete identities are represented by operatic masks, each one identifying individual roles. In today's society, "personality" refers to how one is perceived by others or what a person does professioally. For instance, a missionary father is perceived as a priest. In addition, personality also refers to social status. Thus, specific social status correspond to persons with different professions.

It is a social phenomenon for personality to be perceived through one's profession and status. As such, it must be studied with the social viewpoint and not analyzed as a philosophical issue. However, the root of social status can be traced to the philosophical concept of persona. This can be explained by the fact that the basis of social standing is a person's self. A person is perceived by others through his own "self" by which he gains others' respects.

Once a person gains others' respect, another term applies — integrity. Each person believes he has his own integrity that others cannot insult or denigrate. In the past, young people, workers and women were often placed under the jurisdiction of others. Now, they stress on their own integrity and demand respect from their parents, employers or men.

There exists another type of integrity often shown by young people — personal character. They insist on being different from others, claiming to have a different character, specialties and hobbies. Youth in the United States and Europe who expressed dislike for the enjoyments money can buy opted a return to primitive lifestyles. Thus, ths hippies were born. Nitezsche once talked about the "superior man". Contemporary society gave birth to the women's libbers and political strongmen. The specialties of these people represent their character and express their own selves.

In terms of moral ethics, integrity represents a person's virtues or moral character. Its degree determines the extent of a person's moral upbringing. Thus, a person with good moral character is called virtuous while someone with bad morals is mocked as a person without integrity.

Although the words status, role, character, virtues, and integrity differ in meaning, they are fundamentally based on oneself. Society or persons evaluate a person based on social, psychological and moral standards applied to his words or actions. At the center of this evaluation is an integral and individual person.

Persona in western philosophy is defined by Boetius as "an individual substance of a rational nature." There are two important components in this definition: *rational* and *individual*. Somthing that is not rational cannot have a person. Without it, that something cannot be one. Man is rational and therefore persona is applied to him. God and angels are likewise rational, and therefore also possess persona.

Rationality is a shared concept that may be applied to many concrete beings, at least to men, angels and God. Yet, although rationality is important to the concept of persona, it is not a decisive component. Persona is not determined by rationality but rather by the *individual*. A persona must always be a concrete being. Rationality is realted to nature while individuality is a function of existence. In a substance, nature is not determined by person but by existence. Human beings are human beings. an *individual* refers to this or that man.

Since an individual person is a persona, what when differentiates the individual from the persona? Or are they totlly identical and do not really differ? Theoretically, the individual person is a rational individual, i.e. identical with the persona. Both refer to a person. In reality however, the contents of the two do not totally overlap. The individual person, in reality, refer to a specific person who is integral but whose characteristics are not taken into cnosideration. Persona, on the other hand, in reality stresses on his characteristics. He exists in his own way that is different from others'. In western languages' grammar, they have the first, second and third persons. These refer to individual persons' manner of subsistence, which are dependent on existence. In the legal point of view, persona represents rights. A person is the subject of rights, thus the term "natural person". A group bestowed with rights is called a legal entity. Thus, an individual with a persona must refer to an integral person together with all his characteristics. He exists as an integral person.

Catholic theology pays particular importance to persona in explaining the dogma of the Blessed Trinity. Since persona is not explained ontolgically, God is said to have one nature. His existence is also one or else God will be multiple. But he exists in three ways representing three sets of "interpersonal" relationships among the three persons of the Trinity. These relationship are mysteries of the most unfathomable nature.

Scholastic philosophy of recent years often emphasized three points regarding the persona. First, that the persona is one. This one refers to a living individual, not an abstract concept. It is not made up of component parts, but instead causes components to make up a whole. Second, that the persona is autonomous. It is an independent "self" conscious of itself. Third, that the persona is self-governing. It is the master of its own actions whose objective is itself. From these, we see that persona is a rational individual with an integral manner of existence. This integral manner of existence refers to the three points mentioned above, i.e. an integral life.

Appendices

1. In Greek philosophy, the *unum* is regarded by Plato as a conceptual *one*. The multiple is a sharing of this concept. Aristotle divided unum into two: *logical*, as a phrase to explain a subject; and *substantial*, explaining substance to have four different possiblities. First, as a menas to explain inalienable action. Second, as referring to a substance. Third, as a way to express type. Fourth, as a way to express an indivisible concept.

In explaining the unique character of God, Catholic theologians substantially equate one and being. Truth and Good are likewise equated with being.

Kant stressed one as a category of knowledge while Hegel used one as the starting point of his diagnosis. Contemporary western philosophers often analyze one using mathematics and psychology at tools of their study.

2. Locke discussed identity in Chapter 27 of his essay "*Concerning Human Understanding*". He proposed that identity related with the body's physiological structure. Nevertheless, he admitted that man has a spirit from which comes memory. For him, memory must therefore be part of the concept of identity.

In Book One Chapter 6 of his *Treaties on Human Nature*, Hume proposed the use of psychology to explain human identity. He said that society's substance constantly changes although its remains the same substance all throughout.

3. On Persona:

St. John Damascene said: "Persona is the expression of oneself through one's own actions and characteristics. It is differentiated from the subject's existence." (Dialect. c. 43 in Migne P.G. 94. cal.613)

St. Augustine defined it as: "*Singulus quisque homo, qui.... secundum suam mentem imago Dei dicitur, una persona est et imago Trinitatis in mentem.*" (De Trinitate, XV, 7, 11) (Each person is ratioally the image of God. Persona is the image of the Blessed Trinity.)

Boetius' definition says: "*Persona est nature rationalis individua substantia.*" (An individual substance of a rational nature.) (De duabus naturis et una substantia Christi. c.3 in Migne P.L.64, Col. 1345)

An Evaluation of Traditional Chinese Values

The May Fourth Movement, which began in Peiping on May 4, 1919, and altered the direction of Chinese history, was at first a political movement. Its immediate cause was the Versailles Conference, which forced China to grant to Japan the special privileges Germany has won in Shantung through the use of force. This unfortunate event exposed both the weakness of China and mistreatment by more powerful countries. The ensuing explosion throughout China of student oppsition to the Versailles conference forced all Chinese to re-evalutate the position of China among the nations of the world and to strive, with an unyielding determination, to strengthen the country. This originally political movement, however, soon changed into a movement to reform traditional Chinese thinking. China's failure to deal effectively with the great powers, it was thought, was because of a backward Chinese economy and an out-of-date military. The economy and military were in this condition, it was then said, because China had no science. Finally, there was no science, the argument went, because traditiodnal Chinese thinking looked down on science and technology. Accordingly, the new thinking advocated by the May Fourth Movement was to be scientific. Because science came from the West, it was said that China must give up her traditional philosophy and open her doors to Western science.

Dr. Hu Shih, who is the outstanding representative of the May Fourth Movement, was a philosopher rather than a scientist. He once compared Chinese civilization to a three-wheeled cart and Western civilization to an automobile. The three-wheeled cart runs on brute human strength, whereas the automobile is driven by power created by science. [1] Hu Shih, displaying his respect, called the inventors of

---

(1) Hu Shih, "Tung hsi wen-hua te chieh-hsien *(The Differences between Eastern and Western Cultures)*".
Hu Shih wen-ts'un (*An Anthology of the Writings of Hu Shih, Vol. III.*)

steam and electric power "saints", because their inventions revolution-ized Western life and advance Western civilization. According to Hu shih, scientific discoveries strengthen production. Strong production then develops the economy, and economic development raises the stan-dard of living, science, therefore, not only indirectly influences scho-larly research but also directly influences the life of man. In the West, however, the influence of science on life was gradual because scien-tific research had progressed gradually. Futhermore, the revolution in life brought about by science was also gradual and was based on tradi-tional foundations. Only in Russia, after the Communist Revolution, did a Western country destory the traditions of the past and attempt to build what was to be completely new society. Originally, Russia had little science, and Russian life was backward. The communists were willing to expend all their time and energy to catch up with the industri-alized Western countries, and even used an ideology in the industrial-ized countries — socialism.

In the early years of the Chinese Republic, at the start of the reform movement, everybody wanted to work hard to catch up with Western science. Many Chinese thought that traditional Chinese think-ing and the traditional Chinese way of life represented an inert civiliza-tion on the decline and that this conservative Chinese civilization was more concerned with words than with action. Hu Shih emphasized that the Chinese urgently needed a new self-consciousness, saying, "We must admit that we have been wrong. We need to recognize that we cannot compare with other people. Not only in material culture and industrialization are we behind others but also in political and social morality."[2]   In as much as the youth of China saw themselves as far behind other nations, they discarded traditional Chinese culture, think-ing it of no value whatsoever. In the preface to *A New Look At Chinese Culture*, Liu Tai writes:

---

(2) Ch'ing ta-chia lai chao ching-tzu (*Let's Everybody Look in the Mirror*)," Hu Shih wen-ts'un, Vol. III.

Already thirty or forty years before the Chinese Communist "Cultural Revolution", there was an undercurrent of anti-traditional thought in the minds of modern Chinese. In the 1920s and 30s, the expression "evil remanents of feudalism" was used to describe the political system and social structure of China. "Man-eating ethics" was used to protray traditional human relationships and social customs. And "Confucian shop" was used to characterize basic Chinese thought and beliefs. These expressions were an early hint of what was to develop later. [3]

In the early years of the Chinese Republic, most young Chinese sympathized with the left. They had an illusory yearning for the complete reformation proposed by the Communist Party. But, unlike Russia, China arleady had a long and noble culture. In the battle between Chinese culture and Communism, it will be impossible for five thousand years of tradition to be destroyed, Ultimately, traditional culture will prevail.

After the Chinese government moved to Taiwan, the basic policy was stability, within which a sound economy could be developed. Since then, great progress has been made in economic development, science and technology are now leading us to an advanced stage of industrialization. In the midst of this development, the people in Taiwan are enjoying a high standard of living. The government, therefore, and other segments of society are now turning their attention to the spiritual needs of a society. There is a desire to create a new value system based on a rebirth of Chinese culture.

People from all walks of life, and especially young people, no longer have the same attitude towards Chinese culture which intellectuals of the early years of the Republic had. The present attitude is to re-evaluate traditional culture. There is no intention simply to discard traditional culture, as was done in the past; nor is there any intention just to return to traditional values. The concern, rather, is to re-estab-

(3) Liu Tai, Chung-kuo wen-hua hsin luni *A New Look at Chinese Culture*, Taipei Lien Ching, 1981, p. 12.

lish what is best in traditional culture. This endeavor comes not merely from academic research but also from every kind of lived experience.

Traditional Chinese culture stressed authority; the system of government was monarchical. Today, however, government is democratic. Nevertheless, modern Chinese democracy still stressed authority. Demccracy in China is not exactly the same as American or Western European democracy, where the emphasis is political parties. In this regard, other nations in Asia and recently established countries in Africa are also similar to China. Since the founding of the Chinese Republic, the authority of the leaders has been of central importance to the government.

In traditional Chinese culture, the extended family was fundamental to the social structure. Now, as Taiwan becomes more and more industrialized, the extended family has been abandoned and the nuclear family adopted. Nonetheless, the ideal of having three generations under the same roof still survives. Although the children in a family no longer live together after they marry, the parents still live with a son or daugher and take delight in what has been calld for generations the joy of having grandchildren.

Filial piety was of immense importance in traditional Chinese culture. Modern society in Taiwan, however, emphasizes the individual and his or her freedom. Frequently we hear about the "generation gap". Many young Chinese who have studied in America have lost the traditional notion of filial piety. To remedy this situation, the Ministry of Education has advocated an education which develops respect for parents; it has also instituted a "Parents Month". Society at large, moreover, has enthusiastically responded to ceremonies honoring our ancestors. All of these developemtns help children to understand the relationship they should have with their parents to that they may carry out their responsibilities as children.

Rites and ceremonies were extremely important in traditional Chinese culture. Today there are no official ceremonies for the major events in one's life, except, in the case of funerals, where traditional observances are still followed. A Chinese socity once rich in rites and ceremonies has thus become a society with very few such practices.

Many Chinese feel that in today's world where there are more and more occasions when nations comes together to meet, it is regrettable that China does not have a set of Chinese ceremonies or any specifically Chinese protocol for these occasions.

Ethics was at the core of traditonal Chinese philosophy. In Taiwan today, with most attention going to science, the ethics practiced imitates the ethical system of the West. Traditonal cultural values are facing the prospect of elimination. Nevertheless, because of the experience of the past seventy years on the Chinese mainland, during which, at first, leftist thought advocated complete Westernization and then, later, communism destroyed Chinese traditions, all of which resulted in ever-increasing suffering and ever-growing social chaos, even the communists have now begun to speak of a "Chinese-style communism". Furthermore, the Republic of China, under the leadership of former President Chiang Kai-shek, created on organization to work for the renaissance of Chinese culture. At present in Taiwan, numerous scholarly conferences and publications are discussing how to reform traditional Chinese culture. These activities indicate that traditional Chinese culture is not being rejected; rather, efforts are being made to have traditional culture fit today's world.

Concern for spiritual values is at the heart of traditional Chinese culture. Spiritual values deal with man's soul and man's soul is at the center of the life of the universe. All life within the universe relates to man's soul. The development of man's spiritual life occurs when there is mutual assistance and harmony between the individual, mankind, and all creation. Traditional Chinese culture advocated benevolence, moderation, wholeness of life, and integration between man and nature. These traditional ideas show their tremendous value when seen against the problems created by advances in science and technology. The improper use of science has brought about problems such as environmental pollution and ecological destruction, which have already casued a great threat to the life of mankind. These problems demonstrate that all life within the confusion in politics, economics, and intellectual discourse, on the one hand comes from a totalitarian communism that denies basic human rights, and, on the other, from an always unsatisfied hedonism. In this kind of society, we see a great need for the values of traditional Chinese culture.

A life reflecting traditional Chinese culture must of course take into consideration the demands of contemporary society. Such a life should not reject science, but it should always be remembered that science is not life. Science is rather a means for life and must be appropriately placed within the realm of life. Science should be used to develop life to its fullest; never should life become a slave to science. Indeed, the proper integration of science and life is a major problem facing the renaissance of Chinese culture. Science can stiffen and stultify life. Today, Western man is once again seeking a life that allows for art. The European Renaissance once brought a humanistic outlook to life, when this perspective lost its sense of balance, a scientific view of life was created. Now this scientific view of life has lost its sense of balance, and man is again longing for a humanistic perspective. The spirit and thought of traditional Chinese culture represented by ideas such as moderation, the harmoney of the universe, and the integration of man and nature should bring a sense of balance to the world today and can also help to cultivate a Chinese-style of life for the Chinese, thereby creating a renewed Chinese culture.

The Conflict Between The Christian Eschatological View and Chinese Traditional Culture's View of the Present Life

I. Preface

Christian missionary work in China never stopped since Mateo Ricci arrived four centuries ago. In spite of more than forty years of religious suppression by the communists, the Catholic Church in mainland China is growing stronger everyday. However, the Christian faith has not yet reached upper-class intellectuals, a group of people who call themselves atheists; nor has it become popular among the masses who still adhere to Buddhist and Taoist practices. The reason is not politics. Although the Manchu Emperors repeatedly forbade missionary work, the ban was finally lifted after the Treaty of Nanking was signed in 1840. The communist authorities continue their rejection of religion but allow freedom to some religious activities within certain conditions. Catholicism and Protestantism were rejected in the Early Republican era owing to popular anti-imperialistic sentiments. This was a result of humiliating incidents during the Ch'ing Dynasty involving churches, events which fueled accusations that the latter were imperialists' tools. Later, these sentiments cooled down as succeeding presidents were Christian. Indeed, there exist no ploitical reason why Christianity did not flourish in China. Instead, scholars see cultural reasons.

A common and obvious cultural reason is that Chinese intellectuals are tranditionally non-believers of any religion. In the June issue of "The Journalist", an article on the religious beliefs of Taiwan's political leaders chose the sentence "Chinese Confucians do not have strong ties with spirits" as one of the subtitles. The article claimed that this attitude originated from Confucius himself who said that "One must revere spirits but stay away from them." (Analects) The truth is that Confucius believed in spirits and to a greater extent, heaven. What he was against was the overindulgent practice of consulting oracles during the Spring and Autumn and Warring States periods. He favored showing reverence to spirits but frowned upon over patronizing which he equates with lack of respect. For him, fate is nothing but the reward or punishment for good or evil actions. As long as one does good and avoid evil, there is no need to seek the help of the spirits. Since ancient times, Chinese Confucians always believe that religion is the practice of rites to show reverence to spirits. They abstained from these rites and only followed moral principles taught by the master. When Buddhism and Taoism later became popular in China, Confucians refrained from believing. Some went to the extent of destroying idols in public.

Some scholars propose that the reason behind Chinese intellectuals' rejection of Christianity is the Chinese disbelief of sin and the need to be delivered from it. Confucianists find it hard to accept that Jesus Christ became incarnate and sacrificed himself for man's salvation, an idea they consider incompatible with human dignity.

These two reasons are rooted in Chinese cultural tradition. The two abovementioned ideas are often reflected in Confucian humanistic philosophy as well as in the lives of many Confucians all throughout Chinese history. However, they do not represent fundamental Confucian philosophy at all. From the times of Confucius, the Confucians always expressed "Reverence for Heaven and Respect for Ancestors", a most simple manifestation of religious belief. The basic point of conflict between Confucian culture and Christianity lies in the fact that Confucian humanism stresses values of the present world while Christianity talks about the afterlife. Starting from two different sense of values, two different cultural traditions thus evolved.

II. Christinanity's Eschatological View

When Jesus Christ stated why he came to earth, he said: "I came that they may have life, and have it more abundantly." (Jn. 10:10). The abundant life he meant was eternal life. He also said: "And as Moses lifted up the serpent in the desert, even so must the Son of Man (Jeusus himself) be lifted up, that those who believe in him may not perish, but may have life everlasting.' (Jn. 3:14) These things Jesus spoke, and raising his eyes to heaven, he said: "Father, the hour has come! Glorify thy Son, that thy Son may glorify thee, even as thou hast given him power over all flesh, in order that to all thou hast given him he may given everlasting life. Now, this is everlasting life, that they may know thee, the only true God, and him whom thou hast sent, Jesus Christ." (Jn. 17:1-3)

Everlasting life is not the present life. In fact, they are conflicting. Jesus said to Nicodemus: "Amen, amen, I say to thee, unless a man be born again of water and spirit, he cannot enter into the kingdom of God. That which is born of the flesh is flesh; and that which is born of the Spirit is spirit." (Jn. 3:5) He also told his disciples: "He who finds his life will lose it, and he who loses his life for my sake, will find it." (Mt. 10:39) Thus, losing the present life will lead to eternal life.

St. Paul later stressed these two opposing spirits, besides clearly stating conflict between the two. "Strip off the old man with his deeds, and put on the new, one that is being renewed unto perfect knowledge ' according to the image of his creator.'" (Col. 3:9) "For surely you have heard of him (as truth is in Jesus) that as regards your former manner of life you are to put off the old man, which is being corrupted through its deceptive lust. But be renewed in the spirit of your mind and put on the new man, which has been created according to God in justice and holiness of truth." (Eph. 4:21)

Man was created by God according to his image and likeness, with body and soul. Body and soul form a living person whose life is forever as the soul is spiritual, and therefore enternal. When God created man, he envisaged the human soul according to himself, and destined it to enjoy the True, the Good and Beautiful in eternal bliss. Unfortunately, man's first parents disobeyed God and became His enemies. They lost their right to enjoy the vision of God. In additon, their disobedience left them vulnerable to concupiscence and the tendency to do evil. Evil deserves punishment, the punishment of deprivation of eternal life, or eternal perdition. The symbol of eternal happiness is heaven while that of everlasting suffering, hell. Since hell symbolized eternal death, the world eternal life could only mean everlasting happiness in heaven. Jesus warned his disciples: "And if the eye is an occasion of sin to thee, pluck it out and cast it from thee. It is better for thee to enter into life with one eye, than having two eyes, to be cast into hell-fire." (Mt. 18:9)

Jesus Christ became incarnate, sacrificed his life on the Cross to redeem man from his sins. Thus, he reinstated to man the right to enjoy beatific vision in heaven. Anyone who believes in him and accepts his baptism can partake of this eternal life. That is what Jesus Christ meant when he said that he came to give life abundantly. And those who share in this life is the new man mentioned by St. Paul.

After baptism, a person does not die and enter eternal life right away. He continues living in this world as he did before baptism. However, there is a change in his inner self referred to by St. Paul as spiritual death, which consists in getting rid of the present old man and putting on the eternal new man. Unity with God becomes his objective in life, his sense of values rests on spiritual morality, his desire set on the True, the Good and the Beautiful. St. Paul said: "Therefore mortify your members, which are on earth: immorality, uncleanness, lust, evil desire and covetousness (which is a form of idol worship).... Put on therefore, as God's chosen ones, holy and beloved, a heart of mercy, kindness, humility, meekness, patience." (Col. 3:5, 3:12)

Faith in the eternal life creates a sense of value for the afterlife. As eternal life is spiritual, a sense of value for the afterlife is also mainly concerned with spiritual life. The essence of spiritual life is union with God while the form of spiritual life is obedience to moral law and the fulfillment of religious rites.

This spiritual life targeted towards the afterlife is, in fact, a preparation for eternal happiness in the afterlife. Those who live this spiritual life in the present world will have eternal life in the next word. Eternal happiness consists in enjoying the beatific vision of God. The degree of enjoyment (or the degree of happiness) attained is decided by merits one gained in his earthly life.

> "Do not lay up for yourselves treasures on earth, where rust and moth consume, and where thieves break in and steal, but lay up for yourselves treasures in heaven, where either rust nor moth consumes, nor thieves break in and steal. For where thy treasure is there also will thy heart be..... No man can serve two masters..... You cannot serve God and mammon." (Mt. 6:19, 6:24)

No only should one avoid evil, not even the just riches on earth should he covet. His heart must belong to God. This sense of values produced Catholicisim's religious groups. Men and women all throughout history followed Jesus' summons: "If thou wilt be perfect, go, sell what thou hast, and give to the poor, and thou shalt have treasure in heaven; and come, follow me." (Mt. 19:21). These religious groups are the various religious congregations of men and women of the Catholic Church.

However, man is composed of body and soul. He lives in a material world. Man's body has needs in life, including the desire for enjoyment. Since the material world is a creation of God, then it must be good. Man's needs result from his human nature and are not considered evil. From Christianity's eschatological view, how then should man use the material world to satisfy his needs in life? This issue was discussed in Vatican Council II, the largest meeting held by the Catholic Church this century. Regarding this point, Vatican Council II made the following pronouncement:

" The human entity is made up of body and soul. Corporally, the human body eocompasses the material world. Therefore, the material world reaches its zenith through man. And through man, it offers songs of praise to the Creator. As such, man must not neglect his corporeal life but must acknowledge its beauty and goodness, giving it due importance. The human body is God's creation and will resurrect on the day of judgment. But because of the wounds inflicted by sin, man experiences the disobedience of the flesh. Therefore, human dignity commands that the body should give glory to God and that the body should not be allowed to give in to evil inclinations." (Pastoral Constituation on the Church in the Modern World, Ch. XIX)

This spiritual life can be divided into two: Basic spiritual life consists in daily loving in the world with all its material enjoyments while following moral laws, setting God as the highest goal. This is a way of "giving glory to God within the body" or spiritual life in the world. A higher level of material world is given up. It requires detachment from material goods and following the evangelical counsels: poverty, charity and obedience. Material goods are used only for living needs. This type of spiritual life is "outside" this world.

Lived in the present life, both of these two types of spiritual life have their target set in the afterlife. Doing good and avoiding evil are the means to reach union with God in eternal happiness in the next life.

Man must die to enter eternal life. The good man enjoys eternal happiness while the evil man suffers eternal death. Body and soul separates at the moment of death. The eternal soul will reunite with the resurrected body on judgment day to enter etnernal life.

Thus, in announcing the faith, the Credo of the Catholic Church says: "I believe in .... the resurrection of the body and life everlasting."

III. Traditional Chinese Culture's View of the Present Life

In traditional Chinese culture's view, cosmos is often considered as one single body, an idea derived from the Book of Changes (I Ching). In I Ching, cosmos is viewed to be in a continuous change as affected by yin and yang principles. Heaven, earth and man are the subjects of change while being governed by their specific laws. Heaven, earth and man, collectively called san ts'ai (three matters), represent the whole cosmos. Changes in the cosmos led to the creation of all things. In I Chuan, it says that: "Production and reproduction is what is called the process of change." (Hsitz'u Chuan, Part One, Chapter V). Studies of the I (or change) in the Han Dynasty represented the cosmological change cycle with agricultural intervals in the four seasons, thus: the period of birth, Spring; the season of growth, Summer; the period of harvest, Autumn; and the time of storage, Winter. The I Chuan also said: "The great attribute of heaven is giving and maintaining life. What is most precious for the sage is to get the highest palce. What will guard this position for him? Benevolence." (Hsitz'u Chuan, Part Two, Chapter 1). These concepts of creation and benevolence are necessary and basic to Confucian humanism.

Han Dynasty Confucianists first proposed the idea that ch'i (or material force) led to the creation of all things. Nature was created by ch'i which is divided into the yin and the yang which later separated into five paths while cotinuously undergoing change. Man, also originating from ch'i, changes constantly from birth to old age. Thus, man's life is associated with cosmic nature, both their lives being a result of changes in chi'. Ch'i changes as function of the extreme ebb and flow of the yin and the yang. When these two elements separate, yin becomes the spirit (p'o) to be relegated to earth while yang is transformed into the soul which goes up to heaven. Upon reaching the ch'i in heaven, the soul assumes its original dispersed state. Therefore, we can say that the Confucianists proposed that man lives in the cosmos, originating from the cosmos' ch'i to which it returns after death.

The Book of Songs (Shih Ching) includes elegies dedicated to Wen Wang, praising his soul which people thought resides on God's side. This comes as a result of the Shang and Chou people's belief that their departed kings ascend to heaven, an idea which later led to the practice of offering to ancestors. In later generations, rites of offerings became a common way of showing filial piety. Nevertheless, whether or not souls of ancestors exist after death is a mystery for the Chinese. In fact, there is a Chinese saying which goes: "If only our ancestors in the other life could know!"

Buddhism, which came to China much later, attempted to fill this gap. Buddhism teaches that man reincarnates after death as a reward or punishment. Based on merits and demerits gained in his life, a person has five possible destinies, namely: bliss (or "Western"), man, hell, hungry demon and beast. Reincarnation contiunes until a person is cleansed free of desires to finally reach the state of nirvana. Reincarnation is a process that goes around on earth while nirvana is a state outside this world, reserved for those who deserve it and those who achieved the state of sanctity. Very few are said to reach he state of sanctity as most remain in the reincarnation cycle, and therefore, remain living in the present world. Thus, although Buddhist teaching includes the concept of afterlife, it is only some form of a process in life.

Chuangtzu, a Taoist, proposed the chihjen or chenjen (perfect man). His philosophy extols this perfect man as being able to associate with nature's yuanch'i. They yuanch'i, or the prime matter of the cosmos, is eternal. Because of it, man is also "eternal as heaven and earth". The Taoists believe in the existence of hsienjen (or fairies), eternal beings who do not live on food but subsist on nature's real ch'i. For them, both men and the hsienjen are of the present life, not of the next life.

All schools of thought in traditional Chinese culture view life to be of this present world. Although Buddhism have a notion of the afterlife, they view it only as a continuation of the past, the present and the future.

Enjoying good fortune and avoiding bad luck are what the Chinese usually aspire for in life. Ancient Chinese books classify human sorrows and fortunes as the wufu liuchi (or five fortunes and six extremes). The so-called five fortunes are longevity, riches, well-being, virtues and good death while the six extremes are short life, sickness, sorrow, poverty, evil and weakness (Hungfan). They can be both physical or spiritual but all of them are possible fates in the present life. Mencius once said: "A gentleman has three joys. Not even ruling the world deserves to be one of them. The first is to have both parents living and to enjoy harmony with fellow siblings. The second is to have a clear conscience with heaven and his fellowmen. The last is to acquire talented students to educate." These three joys mentioned by Mencius are but spiritual joys enjoyed in the present life.

Traditonal Chinese sense of values stresses on the spiritual, paying much attention to the life within. The human heart, something spiritual, must be free. In fact, the human heart reflects the heart of nature. Confucians believe that nature possesses creative characteristics. Its very mind is to create. Man, on the other hand, shares this mind of nature. Thus, the human heart is benevolent (Jen). Sung Dynasty's Chu hsi said: "The mind of heaven and earth is to produce and that man and things have received it to be their minds. This mind encompasses everything. And it is nothing else but benevolence itself." (Chuwenkung, Book 67, On Benevolence) "Benevolence is the creation of life." (Chutzu yulei, Book 20) "Benevolence is the form while loving is its application. Or that love is the expression of benevolence. Nevertheless, to explain benevolence, one must not neglect to mention love." (Chutzu yulei, Book 20) From these, we see that Confucian morality is centered on benevolence. According to the Chungyung, the application of benevolence is achieved by "praising the creation of heaven and earth." By being sincere with nature, one praises its creation. (Chapter 22) The model of moral virtues is the sage whose characteristics include "praise for the creation of nature". The Chungyung also said: "Lauding the creation of nature as beyond the heavens is the manner of the sage." (Chapter 27) Thus, the expression of the sage's behavior is what Mencius formulted as: Affection for parents, benevolence to fellowmen and love for creatures (nature). (Chinhsinshang)

Based on its views of the present life, it is proper to say that Chinese traditional culture is a culture of life. Since man's life is everlasting, lasting existence in this present life is desired. Chinese filial piety is a proof that Chinese culture is one of life. As children are the continuation of parents' lives, children's life must consist in acts of filial piety to parents. The purpose of filial piety is to extend the life of parents forever, with an unending generation of descendants to make offerings. Human merits or demerits are likewise transmitted to next generations. As the saying goes: "A meritorious family shall have an overabundance of joy."

Yet man's life can not overcome death. To remain forever and have one's fame preserved, one can achieve great feats in life. The Chinese fear the judgment of history. Since Confucius made judgments on men and events in the Spring and Autumn Annals, everybody became more conscious of how history will judge them after death.

Chinese traditional culture is also a culture of practical life. During his entire life, the Chinese pays attention to his daily life. Unlike the Indians who stress on ideals and mystical life, Confucianism, Taoism and Buddhism base their philosophy of life in practical life. Althought Zen Buddhism forbids publicizing of the path of Zen, and while rocords of Zen masters' dialogues are seemingly illogical and difficult to understand, life in the Zen and of those who attained it consist in ordinary things. The only difference is that they have to rid themselves of worries and achieve spiritual peace. Chinese traditional culture deals with the human way of life, not abstract principles. Although Chuangtzu and the idealists of the Sung and Ming Dynasties proposed principles in form, their purpose still relates with concrete human ways of life. This shows that Chinese philosophy is a pragmatic philosophy of human life, while at the same time not being solely materialistic. In Chinese philosophy, man is of this life, associated with the cosmos and nature. Prime matter is ch'i which undergoes change costantly to cause creation. As such, man seeks for unity with nature, thereby praising the creation of nature.

IV. Conflict and Convergence

In contemporary Chinese intellectual circles, this conflict between traditional Chinese view of the present life with the Christian eschatological view reached its heights during the Early Republican era. Chen Tu-hsin, an advocate of communism, proposed then that "In this world, man is temporary while society is real.... All religion, law, morals, politics are but means to preserve it."[1]   Wu Tzu-hui, who didn't believe in the existence of God, said: " Therefore God spirits....these horrendous terms should better be erased."[2]   He believed that cosmos is a fusion of matter and spirit. It is capable of infinite changes and must be handled with the human brain and "almighty science". Hu shih, known as the guru of contemporary Chinese thought, said: "Based on biology and sociology, we must let people realize that man -- the lesser one -- must die while the human race -- the greater one --exists forever. To let people realize that they must live for everybody is tantamount to religion, the supreme religion. Those that stress "heaven" or "paradise" for the individual are selfish religions.[3]   Ts'ai Yuan-p'ei, another so-called authority on contemporary Chinese education, said: "The issue of the so-called religion is now passe in the west. All issues on religion have been resolved by scholars using science. While in Europe, I saw many people entering churches. But this was only due to historical habits.... What was strange is that no Europeans follow this special practice in China, yet they used facts about their countries' past, disguising them as new knowledge. Many surprisingly discussed the issues and misunderstood preachers' words. All these are attributable to religions views of Chinese Christians. [4]

Such a trend continued for some fifty years at a time when Chinese intellectuals were hurrying to introduce western natural science into China and to reform Chinese society. They believe in the "almighty science" and that science was against religion. After more than forty years of rule of mainland China by the communists, people's life continues to deteriorate, thus highlighting the errors of communism. On the other hand, the search for democracy continues

---

(1) "The True Meaning of Life", "*Ts-shiu Collections,* Vol. 1, p.183.

(2) Wu Tze-hui, "*Universal View, Science and Sense of Values*", Science and Literature, Vol. 2, P.500.

(3) Hu Shih, Science and Sense of values, Vol. 1, P.27.

(4) Ts'ai Yuan-p'ei, "Replace Relgion with Art", *Collection of Chinese Philosophical Thoughts*, Modern Ed. (1), P.359.

everywhere. More and more people turn to study the Chinese classics and Confucianism. Faced with a deprived material life and restrictions on speech and movement, the youths are turning to religion for spiritual appeasement. No matter how much pressure the communist China exerts on religion, the latter continues to spread far and wide. Chinese thought in mainland China follows the so-called Chinese-style socialism. Hung Youlan pushed towards this direction aiming for a breakthrough but he was too enmeshed in Marxist-Leninist socialism. He erroneously veered too much to the left, thus confusing the path of the development of Chinese thought. In the meantime, young philosophers are assiduously promoting Neo-Confucianism.

In stark contrast with mainland China, today's Taiwan is an affluent society. However, it feels a sense of spiritual emptiness amidst material well-being. Society is wanting in moral ethics while persons feel pressure from their material environment. Now, everybody feels the need to return to the spiritual aspects of traditional Chinese culture so as to upgrade the quality of life. While scholars study how to reform Confucian thought, individual person look up to religion for spiritual support. Indeed, Neo-Confucianism and religion are the trends in the development of Taiwan's social thought.

These trends toward Neo-Confucianism and religion both in mainland China and Taiwan differ in terms of content. The people in mainland China believe in religion, deliberately accepting them with all their tradition and organization, with the aim of resisting pressure from communist authorities. Because of this reason, more people choose to join the Catholic church and protestant churches. In Taiwan, people seek religion with the hope of counterbalancing material life with religious spiritual life, with very little attention paid to the contents and organization of religions. Thus, not a few turn to Buddhism. The Neo-Confucian movement in Taiwan will stress benevolence, hoping that it would harmonize individual and community life. In terms of the enjoyment of material goods, democracy and science are the two important ways for its achievement.

Although these incipient trends work in such a way that they avoid conflicts with the Christian faith, harmony with the concept of eternal life remains a problem. The atheism proposed in the past by Wang Tung is still deeply rooted in people's mind. Belief in spirits unwelcome. They only accpet the concept of heaven (shangt'ien). Believing that when a person dies, his souls (hun, p'o) disperse, they reject the idea of transformation into spirits. On the subject of physical resurrection, they would find the idea something to laugh at the way the Athenians reacted when they first heard about resurrection from St. Paul.

In Europe, dramatic changes in the structure of European societies came about as a result of the two world wars. In the last chapter of his book "The Decline of the West" published in 1918, Oswald Spengler wrote: "The dictature of money marches on, tending to its material peak, in the Faustian Civilization as in every other. And now something happens that is intelligible only to one who has penetrated to the essense of money. If it were anything tangible, then its existence would be forever - but, as it is a form of thought, it fades out as soon as it has thought its economic world to finality.... But with this, money, too, is at the end of its success, and the last conflict is at hand in which the Civilization receives its conclusive form -- the conflict between money and blood." [5]

Money has become the target both of governments and private citizens in European societies of this century. Scientific research is aimed at utilizing resources of this world for pecuniary gains. Politics of nations aim to expand markets and get hold of raw materials. At present, European technology and political strength are behind the United State's. The civilization based on money is gradually on the decline.

A society built by a philosophy giving too much stress on money is a vulgar one. Speaking before a symposium on St. Augustine, one

---

(5) Oswald Spendgler, *The Decline of the West*, Alfred A. Knopf, Inc., 1928, Vol. 2, p.506

European scholar likened present conditions in Europe to those of the dark societies in St. Augustine's time. Savage ideas have flooded tradi-tonal civilization. [6]

In the Vatican Council II's Pastoral Constitution on the Church in the Modern World, a deep analysis of present European and U.S. soci-eties was made. It says: "Today the human race is passing through a new stage of its history.... As happens in any crisis of growth, this transformation has brought serious difficulties in its wake. Thus, while man extends his power in every direction, he does not always succeed in subjecting it to his own welfare. Striving to penetrate farther into the deeper recesses of his own mind, he frequently appears more unsure of himself. Gradually and more precisely he lays bare the laws of society, only to be paralyzed by uncertainty about the direction to give it." [7]

> "A change in attitudes and in human structures frequently calls accepted values into question. This is especially true of young people.... The institutions, laws, and modes of thinknig and feeling as handed down from previous generations do not always seem to be well adapted to the contemporary state of affairs. Hence arises an upheaval in the manner and even the norms of behavior. Finally, these new conditions have their impact on religion. On the one hand, a more critical ability to distinguish religion from a magical view of the world and from the superstitions which still circulate purifies religion and exacts day by day a more personal and explicit adherence to faith. As a result many persons are achieving a more vivid

---

(6) Lyndon H. La Rouche, "The Lessons of Augustinian Statecraft for the Contemporary Dark Age of Civilization Saint Augustine", Schiller Institute Conference (Rome), Nov. 1-3, 1985. Nen Benjamin, Franklin House, New York, 1985.

(7) Pastoral Constitution on the Church in the Modern World (Gaudium et Spes), Ch. IV.

sense of God. On the other hand, growing numbers of people are abandoning religion in practice.... presented as require- ments of scientfic progress or of a certain new humanism." [8]

The cultural traditions of both the east and the west are undergo- ing great changes. Struggling under the pain and chaos of attacks and destruction levelled against tradition, they both seek to form a new human civilization based on tradition. Western societies have broken the seals that bind things to religious faith, taking a secular perspec- tive of the events of the present world as they adopt a secularized life. But in maintaining a secular basis, faith in God must be kept. In this way, a final objective for secularized life can be maintained -- return to the source of life and enjoying eternal life. Chinese society has destroyed traditional rites and family systems in its search for dignity and freedom of the individual persona, as well as in its pursuit of the enjoyments of the present world. But the search for traditional humane- ness must be the foundation on which a life of well-being must be built. From humaneness, we touch the human heart which in turn leads to benevolence. With benevolence, we achieve unity with the mind of heaven and earth, thereby fulfilling the "unity of heaven and man" of our traditional culture.

Judging from present trends in both cultures, conflicts between the eschatological view point and the view of the present life still exist. However, in the case of the west, the eschatological view has become so subtly present that it does not form an obstacle to the pursuit of enjoyments in the present life. In fact, with the rationale of fully utilizing the blessing of God, it encourages scientific research. The "heaven" mentioned in Chinese "unity of heaven and earth" refers to God, the Creator. God's creative power is a manifestation of his "mind to produce and reporduce". If we accept that heaven is spiritual and enteral, then unity with heaven would naturally mean enteral life spiritually. This eternal life, neither an illusion nor in conflict with the

---

(8) Ibid., Ch. VII.

present life, is a logical development of the "unity of heaven and man". There certainly will be many components of western culture in the new Chinese culture. Scientific thechnology, individual dignity and freedom will be given much importance. These components, originally associated with the eschatological view, can help Chinese intellectuals accept faith in the afterlife. Indeed, we are optimistic about contact between the Christian faith and Chinese culture. But this optimism requires the entry of the Christian faith into Chinese culture in a way that can be called a life of faith expressed with Chinese culture attributes.

Rapprochement Between Modernized
Confucian Thought and Christian Belief

Can the teachings and spirit of Christ and the thought and spirit of Confucius strike up a relationship?

Is not communist rule, admittedly the representative power of the government in mainland China, outright materialistic atheism? Is not Neo-Confucian thought, the self-styled representative of Chinese traditional culture, the reformed humanism of Confucius, which places religious belief an moral philosophy at a great distance away? Are not the supposedly Christianized nations of Europe now undergoing a process of social secularization, trying to shake off the restraints of Christian doctrines? The situations in the East and in the West are quite different, and yet they are both not conductive to the harmonious rapprochement between Christian teachings and Confucian thought. Under such circumstances, can we speak of the mediation between Christian teachings and Confucian thought? My answer is in the positive.

I. Difficulties from Both Sides

1. From the Confucian Perspective

Ever since the days of Confucius, Confucian thought has been man-centered humanism. The trigrams of the I-ching have three lines: the top line represents heaven; the lowest line, earth; and the intermediate line, man. Man, heaven and earth from the "three powers." Double up the trigrams, and you will have six lines; the six lines are lines of double trigrams. "What makes I-Ching a great book is its vast and comprehensive contents, comprising the way of heaven, the way of man and the way of earth. The "Three powers" are included, and if you double the three, you will obtain six. The six refer to nothing but the Way of the Three powers." (Hsi Tz'u, Section II, Chapter 10)

From "Li-yun" of Li chi:

" Therefore man is virtues found if heaven and earth, the mixing of yin and yang, the meeting of the spirits and the gods, the elegant spirit of the five elements... Therefore man is the heart of heaven and heart, the beginning of the five elements; he had the sense of taste, can distinguish sounds, and can be attracted by color, in a word he has life."

This is to consider man from the aspect of spirit. The spirit of man is the elegant spirit of heaven and earth. The purified spirit or the elegant spirit constitutes man. Man has a spiritually lively heart. The human heart is non-material, and very affective, it has the capacity of knowing and ruling. The Confucianists of the Sung period, like the two Chang brothers and Chu Hsi, conceived of the human heart as coming from the heart of heaven and earth. At the heart of man is jen. Mencius long ago taught that the human heart embrace benevolence (jen), righteousness (yi), propriety (li) and wisdom (chih), the four beginnings. Therefore Confucianism takes it that the human heart has the reasonableness of humanity. The reasonableness of humanity is the principle of human living. The Doctrine of the Mean says: "What heaven has conferred is called the nature; in accordance with this nature is called the path of duty; the regulation of this path is called instruction." (Ch. I)

Human life should go by the reasonableness of human nature, which is called the path of duty. The path of duty is sincerity.

Again, from the Doctrine of the Mean:

" Sincerity is the way of heaven. The attainment of sincerity is the way of men."(Ch. XX, 18)

Confucian philosophy has human nature as the foundation, upon which is constructed a whole system; Confucianism places religious beliefs outside philosophy. Only in the Shu-Ching (the Book of Historical Documents) and Shih Ching (the Book of Poetry) are found discussions on beliefs pertaining to the supreme god. Beliefs of this kind were realized in the supreme gods mandate to the emperor, who followed the Tao on behalf of heaven in governing the emperor on behalf of the multitude at sacrifical places in solemn cremonies. The people faith in heaven above was confined to believing in its administration of reward and punishment. In Confucius' view, reward and punishment by the supreme god are meted out in accordance with man's goodness and evil, respectively. What is required of man is to do good and avoid evil. The criterion for good and evil lies in the innate nature of man and the nature law (tine-li).

Human nature and the natural law are originally begin. The Great Learning says that the Way of Great Learning is "to illustrate illustrious virtue, to renovate the people, and to rest in the highest goodness." Humanity is endowed with inborn virtues, which are naturally transparent. Yet man's heart has selfish concupiscence. Concupiscence covers up human natures shining virtues, so that man cultivation of himself is in the overcoming of selfish desires, thus enabling humanity to shine forth illustrious virtues. The Doctrine of the Mean says: "Sincerity the way of heaven." This is to say that the saints heart is clear and without concupiscence, whereby man's illustrious virtues will naturally become transparent. Hence this is spontaneous sincerity. Men in general, including the sages, have selfish desires, so that they need to overcome their selfishness. Thus it is said, The attainment of sincerity is the way of men".

Cultivation by overcoming concupiscence can be practiced by every one. Thus Mencius said, "man's heart has the four beginnings of benevolence (jen), righteousness (yi), propriety (li) and wisdom (chih)". The four beginnings need to be developed by human efforts. To develop the four beginnings in one's heart, one should try to overcome concupiscence.

People should seek to overcome concupiscence. Overcoming concupiscence is the way of personal cultivation for all people. Everyone should do this, and everyone can achieve it. Lu Hsiang-shan and Wang Yang-ming spoke of "investigating things and extneding knowledge", which is to rectify things until reaching "the natural knowledge of good " (liang-cin), whereby knowledge and action are in unity. The unity of knowledge and action can be attained by all persons. In Confucian thought, there is no such concept as original sin, and there is no thought that human beings need to be redeemed. People do good on their own; human beings are absolutely capable of doing good, and all, by their own efforts, can become sages. Doing good for the Confucians needs no help from heaven above. From the Confucian standpoint, this is a fundamental point of divergence from the Christian faith. At the nucleus of the Christian faith is the redemptive work of Christ, but Confucians would consider that an unnecessary myth. They can believe that Jesus Christ is a great person but do not believe that Christ is the Son of God who descended to earth. Moreover, they do not believe that Jesus Christ is the savior of mankind. Confucian and Christian ethics, however, can find an accord: that is publicly recognized. But, at the present time Confucian ethics is under revision; how much of traditional ethics can be retained is difficult to predict. Filial piety seems to have all but disappeared; Confucius' teaching of emphasizing righteousness and de-emphasizing profit seems to have given way to violent and extreme mass movements; cordial and courteous acceptance seems to have been replaced by the crude behavior of personal attack. Nowadays, speaking to people in Chinese society about the Ten Commandments is apt to be looked down upon as conservative as talking about Confucius and Mencius benevolence, righteousness, propriety and wisdom. Hence if there are probable approximations between Confucian ethics and Christian ethics, such a thought is considered somewhat far-fetched and unrealistic. Furthermore, those who now speak of the reform of Confucian thought emphasize the "non-religious nature" of Confucianism and what Confucian call "the dignity of human nature."

2. From the Christian Perspective

As far as Christian beliefs are concerned, differences in interpretation are legion. In considering the relationship between Christian beliefs and Confucian thought, if I speak as a Catholic Christian, I cannot speak for all the various branches of Christianity represented here. I can only touch upon some of the most fundamental points about the Christian faith.

Even if the Christian religion has many branches, there is still a fundamental consideration, and that is that none is willing to revise one's doctrine so as to accomodate the doctrines of other religions or other philosophies of life. With the Catholic Church this is even more fundamental. During the reign of Kang Hsi of the Ching Dynasty, because of the rites controversies about ceremonies to heaven, to Confucius and to ancestors, the Pope risked administrative error and danger in the Chinese missions by strictly forbidding these rites rather than endanger doctrinal integrity. As a result the links between Catholicism and the Confucian tradition were cut off. Today, other branches of Christianity have the same kind of psychology; they would rather avoid meeting Confucian tradition and Neo-Confucianism than endanger their own dogmas. Hence, in our discussion on the possible rapprochement between Christian beilefs and Confucian thought, we can only go outside the area of dogmas, or we can proceed on condition that we do not harm the Church's dogmas.

Another point, which is fundamental to all Christian denominations, is that their beliefs enter into the various aspects of human existence, whereby private as well as social life are subject to the restraint of Christian convictions. It is not only at times of prayer or praying for blessings and the averting of disaster that Christians believe in God, unlike the Chinese people who express their religious beliefs in terms of relationships with deities with respect to disasters and blessings only. Although Buddhist beliefs include references to future existence, as far as the present life is concerned, Chinese people follow the Confucian tradition and do not make use of Buddhist beliefs. Only in Europe and North American is the social tendency at the present time to narrow the sphere of control of reilgious beliefs, with the result that life and religious beliefs are compartmentalized; however this tendency is not acceptable to all Christian groups.

Still another fundamental tenet is the belief that Jesus Christ is the savior of mankind, that he is God, the Creator of men and women as well as their Redeemer. In the West there are those who place great trust in natural science and oppose religious beliefs. In China today to there are self-styled reform-minded people who claim that science has proven that the universe is not created by God (in this years Youth Day special issue of the Central Daily, so argues a professor of psychology from National Taiwan University). Moreover, Chinese tradition posits that human nature is good at birth and that by their own efforts human beings can attain sagehood, without the need of a divine savior. Although many well-educated Chinese can see that Christ was a great person with an extraordinarily noble character, and although they grant that he was the great founder of a religion, yet a great man is but a person, and a person does not have the status of savior of the world, as Christ is supposed to be.

In terms of ethical values, Christian dogmas, especially from the Catholic standpoint, have fundamental differences from Confucianism. These differences have to do with ontology and transcendence. Chinese philosophers can affirm moral transcendence; they can also recognize the pursuit of spiritual life by human beings, and often speak of "the unity of heaven and humanity." The aim of this knid of pursuit is transcendent, mundane life-denying aim. Yet the transcendence spoken of by Confucians is confined to humanity and the world or human social life and not the nature of man. They think that if human life transcends the nature of man, man loses his humanity, and human life thus has no foundation and is no longer the life lived by persons. On the other hand, Christian beliefs assert that at baptism a person receives the divinity of Christ, i.e. divine life from God. This kind of life comes from the Holy Spirit and is in union with the nature of man at the supernatural level. It does not destroy the life of humanity and elevates the quality and aim of life at the core of the human being. The spiritual life following baptism, with faith, hope and love as dynamic power, is united with God as the direct aim and obtains the value of eternal existence. The dynamic power of faith, hope and love comes from the grace of God. Thus the Christian believers lead their lives at the level of humanity, while in their interior spirits they must overcome sin and move toward god as an activity transcending the realm of the merely human. The variances between the two ways of thinking are not contradictory to each other or mutually exclusive, but are ways of thinking are not contradictory to each other or mutually exclusive, but are on an ascending scale, from the lower to the higher, and are interrelated. The difficulty is in communication at the conceptual level.

That transcendence leads to the life after, and that the life after is eternal life are bound to arouse amazement and doubt in the Confucian but will not lead to denial. The way of filial piety as taught by Confucius requires respect to one's deceased blood relations as though they were living. The hymns to ancestors in the Book of Poetry often refer to the soul of Wang as being by the side of the Heavenly Ruler. While Confucianists of the Han period like Wang Chung denied the existence of the spiritual soul after death, almost all Chinese after Han accepted the Buddhist beliefs of rebirth and hell, so that almost every family invites monks or priests to release the soul of the dead. The Christian doctrine of eternal life does not constitute a difficult point of contact, and it may be a means of reforming social superstition by creating more reasonable and emotional satisfying memorial services of the dead.

II. Mediating Points from Both Sides

Nowadays we Chinese are engaged in considering the modernization of Confucian thought, hoping to see that Confucianism will remain a mainstream of Chinese culture and a model for the life of Chinese. The traditional Confucian model of life is the way of filal piety in the large family, as typified by loyalty to the emperor. Implicit in the way of filial piety is the concept that the fulfillment, or failure, in meeting the requirements of loyalty and obedience will be rewarded or punished, respectively, by the supreme god. On account of filial piety, the Chinese are attached to their native place, and family loyalty and ties among people of the same district are very deep. The traditional model of Confucianism affirms the value of the present existence, and by implication encourages engagement in business to make a living through thrift and endurance of hardship. Although Confucius gave weight to righteousness and made light of profit, although Confucianists of the Han period already had higher regard for agriculture than commerce, yet livelihood in the world requires money, and even if Chinese people do not put the value of money on the same level as knowledge and morality, in the minds of the people in general money occupies a special place. Hence, for the sake of business Chinese people traverse all throhgh southeast China and live in various countries in southeast Asia, holding the economic power of that region. Present-day reform-minded Confucians take worldly existence seriously as well as recognize the importance of money, while family consciousness and district ties will gardually give way to professional organizations as forming the nucleus of society. Concomitant with the value placed on worldly existence and on money is the rise of the pursuit of pleasure. In Taiwan, pleasure-seeking is so prevalent that is has become an important factor in life.

In order, however, to give foundation to new thinking in Confucianism, it is necessary to build up a spititual core, spiritual support, and purpose in life. Many young people in Taiwan are now conscious of spiritual emptiness if their midst, and, coupled with the anguish brought about by the joint examination system, the life of the spirit finds no support and is out of balance. Many youth, then, seek help from religious beliefs; thus more and more young people are now drawn to the study of Buddhism and the study of Christianity. On the other hand, retired old people increase in number, and with nothing to occupy them, they sense spiritual emptiness, and they, too, are motivated to study religion. Reformed Confucians suggest the transcendent ideal of "union between heaven and man." The Confucian ideal of "union between heaven and man," we should realize, needs the "coming together of virtues in heaven and earth." The virtues of heaven and earth are the virtues of respect for life, and that represents the loving heart of the supreme god. On this score Christian belief and Confucian thought find a point of contact. The apostle St. John said, "God is love. " (I John 4:7)

Confucians have the concept that heaven and earth show the virtue of respect for life, which transforms the multitude of things into life, and form a powerful flow of life with the myriad things of the universe, interweaving everything. Wang Yang-ming in "Inquiry on Great Learning" speaks of "jen forming one body".

Jen is life; "forming one body" is the same as "one body of life." Chang Tsai in "Hsi Ming" also says, "Chien (heaven) is father, kuen (earth) is mother.... People are my brothers and sisters, and all things and I are together. "The inter-connection of life in the multitude of things is not only human life united into one body in mutual relationship, but plants, animals and minerals in existence also are infused with life, mutually related. The entire universe is an integral whole, in which all that exist and have life are interdependent and help one another. If one part which exists is damaged to the point that continued existence is threatened, then the entire universe, with the multitude of things in it, is also subject to damage.

Nowadays we are all concerned about the protection of the environment and prevention of pollution; but environmental pollution has reached the alarming stage of threatening the existence of all things in the universe, so that it behooves us to raise our consciousness of this danger and loudly call attention to ecological protection.

We would rather sacrifice economic growth than endanger human existence. This proves what is said in the Bible that God created all things in the universe and allowed human beings to be in charge and see that all things develop properly. The existence of the myriad of things depends of God's love, but human beings betray the loving heart of Creator, squandering so much and upsetting the natural order. We should extol the love which God bestows toward created things, and people should also show love toward the natural order.

Granted that Confucians believe that the nature of man is to "illustrate virtue", and granted that Wang Yang-ming believes that the heart of man is reason, if only man will show forth his innate nature or righteous conscience, man will be perfectly good. Nevertheless, Confucians recognize that the human heart is born with selfish passions and in order to show forth the illustrious virtues of man's nature, and in order to realize the righteous conscience, one must overcome concupiscence. Mencius has said that "to cultivate the heart, nothing is better than having few passions" (Chin-hsin, II). Although Confucians customarily believe that man by his own efforts can overcome selfish passions, yet in actuality we all say, "The heart is more than willing but power is lacking." Therefore we cannot but admit that mankind is afflicated with sin. Hsun-tzu even taught that man is born evil, the Legalists disagreed with Confucius "Government of virtue" and practiced "government by law" through "severe punishment and austere laws". At present, in Chinese society crimes multiply daily, and in Taiwan it is admitted that crimes committed by youth constitute a serious social problem. On the other hand, Confucian scholars are posed to the Christian doctrine of original sin. It should be pointed out that they might not understand the meaning of original sin. They think that original sin destroys what is fundamental in humanity in that it posits man is born evil. Actually original sin means man's opposition to God, for the bad aftermath of original sin is in increasing the effect of concupiscence. As St. Paul says, "But I perceive that there is in my bodily members a different law, fighting against the law that my reason approves and making me a prisoner under the law that is in my members, the law of sin. Miserable creature that I am, who is there to rescue me out of this body doomed to death God alone, through Jesus Christ our Lord! Thanks be to God!" (Romans. 7:22-25) Assuming that we feel keenly that "the heart is more than willing but power is lacking," now that Christ who is sent from above offers his helping hand to the end that we have the power to realize the good that the heart desires, Confucians cannot say that this contradicts human nature and robs man of his dignity. Confucius once said, "When three persons walk, there must be one who can be my teacher." (Shu-erh) Confucians do not consider it shameful to receive instruction and advice from others, then why should they consider it humiliating to obtain divine counsel and help.

The Confucian philosophy of life further can provide the Christian doctrine of salvation a very good explanation. Originals in has been perpetualed by the first man Adam to all mankind. He began the human existence which has been transmitted by natural generation. The human race formed by natural generation there after has inherited this orginal sin which leads to a way of living in opposition to God and with increased passions. Christ came to the world as a man who had a life that was fully human except that he had no original sin and the pernicious influence of original sin. The intergral life of Christ is the union of humanity and divinity. For the sake of saving mankind, Christ let his whole being, which was both divine and human, be transmitted to those who are baptized. Whoever are baptized receive the life of Christ through the Holy Spirit; they are united with Christ, and together become a new race of man. This new mankind constituted by Christ by baptism, has Christ the progenitor and head. The salvation brought about by Christ and its value are not just juridical supposition nor a representative action but a new constitution for mankind. The life of mankind is one. Since through baptism Christ has washed away the pernicious influence of original sin, then whoever has humanity may believe in Christ and receive the new life that comes with baptism. The Confucian claim that the ten thousand beings in the universe are interrelated in life, my explain what the apostle Paul said in Chatper 8 of the Letter to the Romans, that the created universe was enslaved by original sin but that it may enter upon the liberty and splendor of the children of God. Thanks to the new life of mankind, even the multitude of created things can share in one body the life of the sons and daughters of God, according to the proper measure of life in the natural objects. All things in the universe and human beings are interrelated, people and Christ and interrelated, and the whole universe because of Christ belongs to God the Father (I Corinthians. 15:28)

III. Conclusion

Before I conclude this paper, I must confess that I am in no position to decide in what way Confucianism will be modernized. What I said about the point of renewal in Confucianism is based on a Christian point of view. Moreover, it is only fair for me to admit that my point of view is that of a Catholic, which cannot represent all Christian denominations. However, in another sense, the rapprochement between the Christian faith as I have suggested and modernized Confucian ideas may gain the acceptance of both various schools of contemporary Confucian thought and people from various Christian traditions; for what I have said covers several basic points from both sides.

Traditional Confucianists from the rulers Yao and Shun until the end of the Ching Dynasty believed in a Heavenly Lord on High. The Ching emperors made offering to Heaven. In Peiping there is a Temple of Heaven. The common folk believed in reward and punishment by heaven above. At present, while there prevails an anti-religious trend of thought in the name of science, young people and retired old people experience a spiritual vacuum, and they are in search of religious support. At time like this, the Neo-Confucianists suggestion of a Heavenly Lord on High and the Christians belief in God Almightly constitute a point of intersection. Traditional Confucianists conceived of the human heart as jen. Because at the heart of heaven and earth is jen, when the heart of man is in tune with the heart of heaven and earth, man's heart is filled with jen. Jen is the principle of love. Mencious and The doctrine of the Mean conceive of man as having jen. In our society today youth often show their share of cruelty. In mainland China, Communism advocates class struggle. Therefore we deeply appreciate the Confucians reiteration of jen, which is essential to the re-nurturing of love in the Chinese race. The Christian religion has love (jen-ai) at the center. Hence Confucian jen and Christian love from another intersecting point.

Furthermore, Confucians speak of "jen forming one body," which conceives of the whole universe as one body with life flowing through. The natural order and the created things in it as well human beings are interdependent and need one another for their existence. There must not be the devouring of the weak by the powerful, and there must not be the squandering of natural resources to satisfy human greed, otherwise all are doomed. Christian beliefs take the universe and all things in it as Gods creation and ordain man to make good use of them. Moreover, God has set the natural laws, according to which the natural resources can be used for human benefits, and infringement of which will damage both the natural order and mankind. This is also a meeting point between Confucian thought and Christian beliefs. The universe is one and governed by natural law given by the creator.

Whereas Confucians declare that it is in the nature of man to be enlightened about morality and that man by himself can come to this state of bright moral enlightenment, they believe that only the sage, endowed with enlightened wisdom, whose heart and soul are without selfish desires, can themselves" illustrate illustrious vitrues". Thus when Confucians say, "Sincerity is the Way of Heaven," they mean that only the sage can naturally achieve utter" sincerity to do [what they set out to do], for their is the way of man." That is to say, we all need to endeavor to overcome selfish desires. However, the natural-born sage has not appeared. Even Confucius himself confessed, not until he reached seventy did he come to the point of "following what the heart desires and not trespassing what is proper." The Confucian sage is one who is without original sin. Only Christ, and Christ's mother, Mary, are also without original sin. This serves as a final point of rapprochement. Mankind needs redemption.

The Religions of Asia

We read from the book "Our World's Heritage" that all the so-called human heritage belongs to the realms of the royal and the sacred. In Europe, we have the architecture of Greece, Rome and those of the Middle Ages. In Asia, we have the temples and shrines of Persia, India, Thailand, Japan and China. These do not only provide tourists a chance to enjoy ancient art but also serve as materials for the study of world culture. "The domes of the Pantheon in Rome and the Hagia Sophia in Istanbul, both designed after the sky, are best examples of how building technology is applied to religion. One can not help but feel a sense of fear and reverence upon entering these shrines. It is as though one is standing at the summit of a mountain of a serene, starlight night."[1] Similarly, travellers also feel a sense of relief upon visiting temples built on the five famous mountains of China or Shinto shrines in Japan. In India and Thailand, temples project a sense of religion that is deeply rooted in people's daily life.

Indeed, reilgion is very much a part of the Asian way of life. That is because Asia is the cradle of the world's religion. Aside from the ancient religions of the Persians, existing religions such as Judaism, Catholicism, Hinduism, Buddhism, Islam, Taoism and Shintoism originated in Asia to form the world's culture spheres. Countries in Europe and the Americas belong to the Christian cultural sphere. Islamic countries include those in Asia Minor, North Africa, Southeast Asia and Pakistan. Sri Lanka, Burma, Thailand, China, Veitnam and Japan together form the Buddhist cultural sphere. India has its own Hinduism cultural sphere. In these cultural spheres, religion still forms part of people's lives, not a relic of history. In fact, religion takes the center stage in some of these people's daily life.

---

(1) *Our World's Heritage*, Chinese Edition, Chinhsiu Publications. p.93.

The religion of India is an ancient one. The sammitas and the Brahmanas are religious texts written more than a millennium ago. Decorated with carvings both in its interior and exterior, the Kailasa Temple in Ellora was hewn out of a cliff in the 7th and 8th Centuries. Yet, in the life of modern day Indians, "Hinduism is reflected in the social and religious aspects of life as 85% of the country's population still practise the religion. Undoubtedly, it forms the cultural basis of people's life." [2]

Buddhism originated in India where many of its ancient cave temples and pagodas still stand today. The Ajanta is a fine example of ancient Buddhist art. Yet, Buddhist religious life prospered outside India in the Buddhist centers of Sri Lanka, Thailand, and Tibet, In Bangkok, the captial of Thailand, roof of temples glimmer under the sun, earning the city the name "Golden City". Monks dressed in bright saffron robes are a common sight in the streets. Upon reaching the age of twenty, boys leave their homes to live the life of a monk for at least three months in a Buddhist temple. In Thailand, buddhism is the bridge between society and the government. Governed by the Dalai Lama and the Panchen Lama, Tibet is a place where religion and state overlap. Despite persistent political pressure from the Chinese Communists, the Tibetans have not changed their attitude.

In China and Japan, Buddhism is a folk religion which influences all aspects of people's lifestyle. Reincarnation and the concepts of reward and punishment are deeply set in the hearts and minds of men. Serene atmosphere in the temple and philosophical discipline reflected by Buddhist texts attract many persons of high learning. In spite of present day economic prosperity, Buddhism continues to draw followers. Zen Buddhism's meditation is a practice aimed at achieving interior peace.

Islam started in Asia Minor. During its heyday, Islam's influence reached as far as Italy and southern Spain. Today, it remains the reli-

---

(2) Nancy Wilson Ross, *Three Way of Asian Wisdom*, Simon and Schuster, 1966 ed., p.14.

gion of the Arabs, as well as of Indonesia and Pakistan. Every year, millions of pilgrims flock to the Holy Shrine in Mecca. In these countries, the Koran is the code of conduct for both the state and the people. Prayer five times a day and observation of Ramadan fast are routine practices. With a firm religious faith and bounded together by a strong sense of unity, followers of Islam rarely convert to other beliefs.

Judaism is the religion of Israelis. After the state's destruction in World War I, Jerusalem became the bone of contention between the Catholics and the Moslems, Judaism almost died. However, the faith continued in the U.S. and the Soviet Union. When the Jewish state was established, Judaism returned to Palestine. Jews do not culturally mix with other races, for the past two thousand years, religion is the spiritual cord that binds the Jewish people together.

Catholicism originated from Judaism. It spread from Jerusalem to Rome, from which it later expanded to become the dominant religion in Europe and the Americas. In Later centuries, Protestantism branched out of Catholicism. Later, Protestantism divided into many sects. In Asia, Catholicism and Protestantism are taken as western religions owing to their identification with the culture of the west.

In the east Asian countries of China, Vietnam, Japan and Korea, Confucian thoughts wield a strong influence. Principally a school of philosophy, Confucianism conceals religion which itself. Confucians profess no concrete religious beliefs although they "revere Heaven and respect ancestors". Confucianism coexist as with other religions. Thus, a person or family may take part in Buddhist, Taoist or Shinto religious rites as chances allow. Nevertheless, it does not consider religion as absolutely necessary. Neither does it favor or object to the practice of religion. As such, religion hardly fares much in Confucian cultures. [3]

I have just briefly described the religions of Asia. Now, let me explain two important points.

---

(3) Ninian Smart, *The World's Religious*, Cambridge University Press.

First, that the religions of Asia have overlapped with Asian cultures. These cultures are ancient ones such as those of Hinduism, Buddhism, Islam and Confucianism. These religions have become part of the people's daily life. Proper religious rites are observed in important events such as birth and marriage and during time of illness and death. Religious events are also included in social and community activities. Religious leaders direct political issues. In addition, other aspects of people's life as cultural heritage, philosophical ideas, morality and art are inseparable from their religions. Only in the Confucian culture is this phenomenon unobservable. Although Asia belongs to one continent geographically, it exhibits cultural diversity owing to differences in race and religion.

In the west, Catholicism and Protestantism have likewise fused with western culture. European and American cultures, basically identical, are Christian in nature. It was only in the last two centuries when western social life gradually diverted from the Christian faith. When Christianity reached Asia, cultural differences and political reasons led to the erroneous idea that it was a type of cultural invasion. Christianity was rejected by the learned class in China. Christian churches in Asia tried contacts between religions, but Asian religions have old and long histories, aside from their high level of culture. Different from the native religions of Africa characterized by low cultural level, they are not easily taken over by the Christian religion despite the latter's high cultural level. It was easier with the native religions of the Taiwan aborigines or the crude religions of the various uncivilized tribes of Europe during the fall of the Roman Empire. Contacts among Christianity and Asian religions must not be religious as it will be rejected by the latter. When the Spaniards conquered the Philippines, the inhabitants of that country have not yet formed part of the cultural spheres of the important Asian religions. It absorbed Catholicism to become the only Catholic country in Asia. Christian churches made contacts with Asian peoples in an individual manner. Those who accepted the faith did so individually, not as a community of family. Many of the Christians in Taiwan are the only one in their own families. After three of four centuries of encounter, the number of believers remained very small, making up only a very small percentage of the local population.

Secondly, that is the policy of the Roman Catholic Church to adopt cultural encounter, not contact between western and native Asian cultures. In this manner, the Church fuses with native cultures by itself without the exterior appearance of western culture. In this way, a single cultural entity is formed with native Asian cultures. The Roman Pontiffs repeatedly directed Fu Jen University to take this task of cultural formation, a task comparable to the Catholic Church's fusion with Greek and Roman cultures to create European culture. But conditions are not the same now. By the Middle ages, the empires have destroyed ancient Greek and Roman cultures. Europeans were converted to the Catholic faith which absorbed Hellenic and Roman traditions. Asian cultures are presently undergoing restoration and rebirth. In contrast with Greek and Roman cultures, these Asian cultures are well preserved and vibrant. In addition, Christians are a minority in these countries. How then can Christian culture be created in these Asian countries?

How the Christian faith can take root in Asia and how Christians can avoid living in the peripheries of their traditional culture while seeking a cultural setting for the living their own faith are issues related to local theology and the acculturation of Catholicism.

Theologically, Asian religions (Hinduism, Buddhism, Taoism and Shintoism) have a weak and hazy concept of God. Hinduism's Vishnu and Khrisna and Buddhism's deity (Buddha) are attributed with creative power and supernatural character. Chinese Confucian's heaven is the universal creator with a unique and spiritual nature. These religious elements can be adopted into Christian theology. However, Asian religions view their gods as an eternal flux. When elevated to a supernatural level, this idea of an eternal flux leads to the concept of mystical life, at once moving and at rest, unlimited and eternal. The mystic life of Hinduism led to the practice of yoga while Chinese Zen Buddhism came up with transcendental meditation to establish Asian religions' special characteristics. They contributed to the formation of the Asian human character. At present, scholars in Europe and the United States are engaged in the study of these mystical religious characteristics. Their youth study yoga and meditation thereby popularizing oriental mysticism. This mystical life has likewise attracted the attention of Protestant and Catholic theologians. They view it in connection with mystical movement now popular among the Christian faithful. These movements invoke the Holy Spirit to move the hearts of the faithful. With prayer, spiritual and mystical union is achieved during which mystical charisma is emanated. Therefore, Asian religions can provide many rich elements to Christian Spiritual life.

Viewed according to the moral point of view, we can likewise adopt the moral teachings of Hinduism, Buddhism, Taoism and most especially, Confucianism into Christian morality.

We have a long way to go in establishing Christian culture in Asian countries by way of acculturation through encounter between Christianity and Asian religions. To fulfill this task, we need appropriate leaders and above all, the guidance and help of Almighty God.

La Voie D'enfance Et La Piété
Filiale Confucéenne

I. La Voie D'enfance

La spiritualité de sainte Thérèse de l'Enfant-Jésus peut se résumer en un mot: l'amour. Sa caractéristique est d'aimer Dieu-Père comme un enfant aime ses parents. Thérèse donne à cette spiritualité le nom de *voie d'enfance*.

> Jésus se plaît à me montrer l'unique chemin qui conduit à cette fournaise Divine, ce chemin c'est l'abandon du petit enfant qui s'endort sans crainte dans les bras de son Père. [1]

A travers l'histoire, tous les saints enseignent comment se sanctifier: les uns quittent le monde et vivent dans le désert; d'autres se cachent dans un monastère, y observant jeûnes et mortifications; certains se consacrent au service des autres; d'autres enfin mènent une vie silencieuse et contemplent Dieu. Thérèse expérimente sa faiblesse physique et, ne pouvant faire siennes les grandes mortifications, elle cherche une méthode simple et adaptée à ce qu'elle est.

> Le Bon Dieu ne saurait inspirer des désirs irréalisables, je puis donc malgré ma petitesse aspirer à la sainteté; me grandir, c'est impossible, je dois me supporter telle que je suis avec toutes mes imperfections; mais je veux chercher le moyen d'aller au Ciel par une petite voie bien droite, bien courte, une petite voie toute nouvelle. Nous sommes dans un siècle d'inventions, maintenant ce n'est plus la peine de gravir les marches d'un escalier, chez les riches un ascenseur le remplace

---

(1) Ms B . lr°

avantageusement. Moi je voudrais aussi trouver un ascenseur pour m'élever jusqu'à Jésus, car je suis trop petite pour monter le rude escalier de la perfection. Alors j'ai cherché dans les livres saints l'indication de l'ascenseur, object de mon désir et j'ai lu ces mots sortis de la bouche de la Sagesse Eternelle: Si quelqu'un est Tout Petit, qu'il vienne à moi. Alors je suis venue, devinant que j'avais trouvé ce que je cherchais. [2]

Thérèse a découvert sa petite voie, et elle s'élance vers le bon Dieu avec un coeur d'enfant. *Cette petite voie* est très simple: l'enfant aime ses parents d'un amour inné, sans raisonnement ni détour, sans chercher pourquoi ni comment. Un enfant de quatre-cinq ans est plein de simplicité: il dit ce qu'il pense, demande ce dont il a besoin, refuse ce qu'il n'aime pas. C'est précisément cette simplicité que les parents aiment. Si au contraire l'enfant n'a pas ce coeur candide, ses parents ne savent comment le prendre. Thérèse aime Dieu avec un vrai coeur d'enfant:

> En dehors de l'Office divin que je suis bien indigne de réciter, je n'ai pas le courage de m'astreindre à chercher dans les livres de belles prières, cela me fait mal à la tête, il y en a tant!.... et puis elles sont toutes plus belles les unes que les autres.... Je ne saurais les réciter toutes et ne sachant laquelle choisir, je fais comme les enfants qui ne savent pas lire, je dis tout simplement au Bon Dieu ce que je veux lui dire, sans faire de belles phrases, et toujours Il me comprend. [3]

> Je devrais me désoler de dormir (depuis 7 ans) pendant mes oraisons et mes actions de grâces; eh bien je ne me désole pas....je pense que les petits enfants plaisent autant à leurs parents lorsqu'ils dorment que lorsqu'ils sont éveillés, je pense que pour faire des opérations, les médecins endorment leurs malades. Enfin je pense que: "Le Seigneur voit notre fragilité, qu'il se souvient que nous ne sommes que poussière. [4]

---

(2) Ms C, 2v° -3r° .
(3) Ms C, 25r° .
(4) Ms A, 75v° .

Par sa psychologie, l'enfant sait profiter de la bonté de ses parents qui, non seulement ne le lui reprochent pas, mais s'en montrent heureux. La voie d'enfance nous enseigne à avoir une telle attitude, car c'est certainement ainsi que nous recevrons l'Amour de Dieu.

L'enfant possède toujours cette confiance totale. Jésus nous dit:

Quel est d'entre vous l'homme auquel son fils demandera du pain, et qui lui remettra une pierre? ou encore, s'il lui demande un poisson, lui remettra-t-il un serpent? Si donc vous, qui êtes mauvais, vous savez donner de bonnes choses à vos enfants, combien plus votre Père qui est dans les cieux en donnera-t-il de bonnes à ceux qui l'en prient! [5]

Thérèse a parfaitement compris cet enseignement. Aussi sa confiance en Dieu est sans limite, et elle se montre disposée à accepter tous les vouloirs de Dieu; elle ne doute pas que Dieu ne veut que son bien. Elle déclare que même si elle avait beaucoup péché, elle ne perdrait pas confiance:

On pourrait croire que c'est parce que je n'ai pas péché que j'ai une confiance si grande dans le bon Dieu. Dites bien, ma Mère, que, si j'avais commis tous les crimes possibles, j'aurais toujours la même confiance, je sens que toute cette multitude d'offenses serait comme une goutte d'eau jetée dans un brasier ardent [6].

Cette confiance, pure et vraie, plaît beaucoup à Dieu. Touchés par la confiance filiale, les parents prennent encore plus soin de leurs enfants et vont même au-devant de leurs besoins non exprimés. Ainsi agit Dieu. Jésus nous dit:

Votre Père sait bien ce qu'il vous faut avant que vous le lui demandiez.[7]

---

(5) Mt 7,9-11.
(6) CJ 11.7.6.
(7) Mt 6,8.

Ce qui afflige le plus les parents, c'est le refus que leurs enfants opposent à leur amour, surtout que ce refus implique un sentiment d'ingratitude. Thérèse a senti ce qui déplaît au bon Dieu et ce qui le fait "souffrir": les hommes ne le connaissent pas et refusent son Amour. Pour réparer cette offense, Thérèse ouvre son coeur en priant le Père d'y verser tout l'Amour refusé par les hommes; elle s'offre en victime à l'Amour pour en être consummé.

> O mon Dieu! votre Amour méprisé va-t-il rester en votre Coeur? Il me semble que si vous trouviez des âmes s'offrant en victimes d'holocaustes à votre Amour, vous les consumeriez rapidement, il me semble que vous seriez heureux de ne point comprimer les flots d'infinies tendresses qui sont en vous.... (....) Ma Mère chérie, vous qui m'avez permis de m'offrir ainsi au bon Dieu, vous savez les fleuves ou plutôt les océans de grâces qui sont venus inonder mon âme..... Ah! depuis cet heureux jour, il me semble que l'Amour me pénètre et m'environne, il me semble qu'à chaque instant cet Amour Miséricordieux me renouvelle, purifie mon âme et n'y laisse aucune trace de péché. [8]

La voie d'enfance se caractérise par cet amour: être aimé par Dieu et l'aimer en retour de tout son coeur, et cela même à la place des autres. Thérèse demande d'autant plus à recevoir cet Amour que les hommes le refusent; elle veut aimer encore davantage parce que les hommes aiment moins. Supposons une famille de huit enfants dont tous sauf un la quittent par ingratitude. Le seul enfant restant aimera ses parents à la place des autres. L'amour de Thérèse envers le Père fait en quelque sorte penser à Meng-tzeu (Meng-tzeu est le premier rcrivain de talent de l'école confucéenne) [9] qui voulait pour lui-même un esprit immense, remplissant le monde, et capable d'aimer toute l'humanité. Thérèse voulait être tous les membres de l'Eglise. Elle comprit que l'Amour était sa vocation, car l'Amour réalise tout:

---

(8) Ms A, 84r° .

(9) Vers 372-389 av. J.-C.

Je compris que si l'Eglise avait un corps, composé de différents membres, le plus nécessaire, le plus noble de tout ne lui manquait pas, je compris que l'Eglise avait un Coeur, et que ce Coeur était brûlant d'Amour. Je compris que l'Amour seul faisait agir les membres de l'Eglise (....) Je compris que l'Amour renferme toutes les vocations, que l'Amour était tout, qu'il embrassait tous les temps et tous les lieux....en un mot, qu'il est éternel!....[10]

Cet amour ne peut venir que d'un enfant; en effet un enfant est seul capable d'une telle sincérité pure et spontanée. Et en même temps cet amour est un acte de haute valeur et de grande efficacité car il ne cherche que la gloire de Dieu, et il est prêt à aller jusqu'à l'effusion du sang.

Ah! malgré ma petitesse, je voudrais éclairer les âmes comme les Prophètes, les Docteurs, j'ai la vocation d'être Apôtre.... Je voudrais parcourir la terre, prêcher ton nom et planter sur le sol infidèle ta Croix glorieuse, mais, ô mon Bien-Aimé, une seule mission ne me suffirait pas, je voudrais en même temps annoncer l'Evangile dans les cinq parties du monde et jusque dans les iles les plus reculées.... Je voudrais être missionnaire non seulement pendant quelques années, mais je voudrais l'avoir été depuis la création du monde et l'etre jusqu'à la consommation des siècles....Mais je voudrais par-dessus tout, ô mon Bien-Aimé Sauveur, je voudrais verser mon sang pour toi jusqu'à la dernière goutte....

Le Martyre, voilà le rêve de ma jeunesse, ce rêve il a grandi avec moi sous les cloîtres du Carmel.... Mais là encore, je sens que mon rêve est une folie, car je ne saurais me borner à désirer un genre de martyre.... Pour me satisfaire, il me les faudrait tous....[11]

---

(10) Ms B, 3v° .
(11) Ms B, 3r° .

L'authenticité de son amour vient de ce que Thérèse veut faire tous les vouloirs de son Bien-Aimé. Elle est tellement remplie de zèle qu'elle voudrait accomplir pour le Père tout ce qu'il est possible de faire à travers le monde. Mais ce zèle est une folie: elle ne peut pas tout réaliser. Tout homme qui veut travailler pour le Père, le fait normalement avec une bonne intention. Thérèse sait bien qu'il lui est impossible de tout faire concrètement, mais elle garde au fond de son coeur le désir de tout réaliser. Elle fait sien l'amour du monde entier car son coeur est sans limites et peut tout contenir. En voulant, par amour, tout faire pour le Père, c'est comme si elle faisait réelement toutes choses, car son amour embrasse non seulement les autres, mais encore toues les action des autres:

> Je compris que l'Amour renfermait toutes les vocations, que l'Amour était tout, qu'il embrassait tous les temps et tous les lieux.... en un mot qu'il est éternel!....[12]

Amour le plus vivant qui soit, le plus positif, car rien n'est pour soi, tout est pour Dieu!

Thérèse imite là l'amour de Jésus pour son Père. Le Fils s'est fait homme pour attirer tous les hommes au Père.

Comme à l'image du Père, il manifeste l'amour du Père; car le Père est Amour, il aime tous les hommes comme le soleil qui illumine chacun sans distinction; comme le Père de la parabole reçoit avec joie le fils prodigue, ainsi le Père céleste, dans son amour, accueille avec bonté tous ceux qui reviennent vers lui.

Comme représentant de l'Humanité, le Christ aime le Père de tout son coeur. La volonté du Père est sa nourriture. Il prêche selon ce qu'il entend auprès du Père; il fait tout ce qu'il voit faire le Père; il ne cherche que la gloire de son Père, jamais la sienne propre. Il obéit jusqu'à offrir sa vie pour le salut du monde.

La vie de Jésus se résume en un seul mot: l'Amour. Il est venu

---

(12) Ms B, 3v°.

en ce monde pour aimer le Père, et c'est encore par amour qu'il est mort. C'est pourquoi le Père a déclaré deux fois que Jésus est le Fils bien-aimé.

Par le baptême, les fidèles ne forment qu'un seul corps avec le Christ, et deviennent fils adoptifs du Père. C'est donc avec un amour véritable qu'ils doivent aimer le Père. En ressemblant à Jésus, Thérèse aime le Père d'un amour filial. Connaissant sa petitesse, elle n'aspire pas aux grands exploits, mais se contente de faire plaisir au Père par des actes d'enfant. Son amour est donc celui d'un enfant: simple, authentique, empreint de confiance. Thérèse veut tout faire pour l'amour du Père.

II. La Piété filiale Confucéenne

La pensée morale de Confucius se résume en un mot: l'humanité (au sens de bienveillance). Elle consiste à aimer la vie, notre propre vie, celle de tous les hommes, la vie de l'univers. Les confucéens vivent l'humanité par la pratique de la piété filiale qui comprend concrètement toutes les vertus. Dans les *Entretiens de Confucius*, Lou Tzeu (un disciple de Confucius) dit:

> L'affection envers nos parents et le respect envers ceux qui sont au-dessus de nous sont comme la racine de la vertu. [13]

Meng-tzeu dit à son tour:

> L'affection envers les parents est un effet de la bienveillance. [14]

La piété filiale apparaît donc dans la civilisation chinoise comme un sommet très caractéristique. L'ouvrage bien classique, qu'est La Piété, débute par cette phrase:

---

(13) Hio Eul; cf. Les quatre livres de Confucius, traduction intégrale, notes et préface du P. Séraphin couvreur, s.j., Paris, Jean de Bonnot Editeur, 1981, P.71.

(14) Tsin Sin; cf. Les quatre livres, p.613.

Là piété filiale est la base de la morale et de l'éducation.

Deux livres de Confucius, les Entretiens et l'Invariable Milieu, traitent des vertus de base: la prudence, l'humanité et la force. Meng tzeu, lui, parle de quatre vertus fondamentales: l'humanité, la justice, la civilité (ou l'urbanité), la sagesse. Les confucéens de la dynastie Han comptent cinq principes: l'humantité, la justice, la civilité, la sagesse et la fidélité. Ces différentes énumérations montrent que, pour tous, l'humanité (ou bienveillance) est le premier fondement. Autant *Meng tzeu* que *l'Invariable Milieu* disent:

La vertu d'humanité est ce qui fait l'homme. [15]

L'humanité est l'amour de la vie; toutes les autres vertus trouvent en elle leur racine. Aimer la vie revient à aimer la source de la vie, que sont les parents. L'amour des parents est donc la racine de toutes les vertus. L'éducation chinoise commence toujours dans la famille ou auprès d'un maître choisi par plusieurs familles; les enfants y sont formés à la piété filiale et au respect envers les aînés. Cette piété filiale confucéenne, basée sur la vie, enseigne aux enfants que leur vie provient de leurs parents; et même, elle ne fait qu'un avec la vie de leurs parents; le corps des enfants sont considérés comme le corps continus des parents. Zen tzeu le dit ainsi:

> Le corps des enfants ne fait qu'un avec le corps des parents. On agit toujours avec le corps de ses parents; oserait-on le faire sans respect!
>
> ne pas se comporter correctement, même lorsqu'on est seul;
>
> être infidèle vis à vis de l'empereur;
>
> ne pas assumer ses fonctions avec respect;
>
> ne pas tenir ses promesses envers ses amis;
>
> combattre au front sans courage;
>
> tout cela est manquer de piété.

---

(15) Invariable Milieu, Ch. 20; Meng-tzeu, Tsin Sin, cf. Les quatre livres, p.637.

Même l'empereur, s'il n'arrive pas à remplir ses devoirs, porte tort à ses parents; alors, qui oserait ne pas pratiquer la piété filiale! (Liki, chiyi)

Les enfants doivent vivre en fonction de leurs parents; faire le bien est piété, agir mal va contre la piété.

Zen-tzeu m'a dit ce qu'il avait entendu proclamer par Confucius: de tout ce que le ciel a fait naître et la terre a nourri, l'homme est le plus grand. Mais la vie de l'homme vient tout entière de ses parents, aussi doit-il tout leur rendre (liki, le Sacrifice).

La vie et le corps des enfants viennent donc des parents; les parents représentent le "Ciel" qui est comme une mère engendrant tout, y compris les enfants. Ceux-ci ont le devoir de prendre soin de leur corps et de leur vie qui appartiennent et aux parents et au Ciel. Toute la vie des enfants est donc orientée en fonction des parents. Zen-tzeu dit:

La piété a trois degrés: le plus haut consiste à vénérer les parents; le deuxième revient à ne pas les déshonorer; le troisième demande de les nourrir (Liki, le Sacrifice).

Les enfants font le bien pour honorer les parents, évitent le mal pour ne pas les couvrir de honte, les nourrissent pour leur assurer une vie heureuse. Le livre de *La Piété* dit:

Il faut tenir ferme dans la pratique de la vertu pour avoir une bonne réputation. [16]

Les enfants étudient pour se former une personnalité, puis développent leurs connaissances pour apprendre comment se comporter: il s'agit d'abord d'être plein de bonté dans le milieu où l'on vit, puis

---

(16) Le livre de La Piété, premier chapitre.

sage dans sa nation. On devient ensuite rhéteur, et encore éducateur, selon le mot: "Pour former les autres, il faut être formé soi-même; pour enseigner les autres, il faut etre savant soi-même." La dernière étape consiste à devenir haut-fonctionnaire, pour oeuvrer grandement au bénéfice de la Patrie, élargir la renommée de son propre nom et obtenir une haute dignité. Tout cela honorera le nom des parents. Ainsi est accomplie la piété. *L'Invariable Milieu* dit:

> Que la piété filiale de Chouenn fut remarquable! Il fut doué de la plus haute sagesse, obtint la dignité impériale, posséda toutes les richesses comprises entre les quatre mers; ses ancêtres ont agréé ses offrandes; ses descendants ont perpétué sa race. [17]

> Quelle n'était pas l'étendue de la piété filiale de Ou wang et de Tcheou koung! Ils savaient admirablement poursuivre les projets et continuer les oeuvres de leurs pères. Au printemps et en automne, ils nettoyaient et préparaient la salle des ancêtres; ils exposaient rangés en ordre les objets et les vêtements dont leus pères s'étaient servis; ils leur offraient les mets et les fruits de la saison. (....) Leur rendre les mêmes devoirs après leur mort que pendant leur vie, après qu'ils avaient disparu que quand ils étaient présents; c'était la perfection de la piété filiale. [18]

Remplir le devoir de piété est, pour les enfants, de première importance. Cela passe au-dessus de tout et reste un souci de toute la vie. Les enfants doivent être parfaits, tant dans leurs paroles que dans leurs actions. Ils gagnent ainsi le respect des autres, d'abord à leur profit, mais également à celui de leurs parents. Plus hautes seront les vertus et la renommée des enfants, plus hautes seront celles des parents. C'est ainsi que les enfants accomplissent leur responsabilité à l'égard de la piété. Chouenn, revêtu de la dignité impériale, sert ses

---

(17) Tchoung Ioung, Ch. 17; cf. Les quatre livres, p.39.
(18) Ch. 19; cfl Les quarte livres, pp.41-43.

parents comme un empereur; c'est pourquoi il est appelé: celui qui eut la piété suprême. Ou wang et Tcheou koung ont poursuivi les projets de Wen wang, et ont gouverné le pays avec humanité et sagesse. Par là leur piété s'est révélée immense. Confucius dit:

> Si durant trois ans après la mort de son père, un fils imite sa conduite en toutes choses, on pourra dire qu'il pratique la pi été filiale.[19]

Les confucéens attachent une grande importance à la vie de l'esprit. C'est pourquoi ils enseignent que la vertu d'humanité est ce qui distingue l'homme de tous les autres êtres. La piété filiale consiste à servir les parents, spirituellement par l'acquisition de l'honneur et de la renommée (cela augmente leur gloire), et aussi matériellement en rendant leur coeur joyeux. Confucius dit:

> La piété filiale qu'on pratique maintenant ne consiste qu'à fournir le nécessaire aux parents. Or, les animaux, tels que les chiens et les chevaux, reçoivent aussi des hommes ce qui leur est nécessaire. Si ce que l'on fait pour les parents n'est pas accompagné de respect, quelle différence met-on entre eux et les amimaux? [20]

L'esprit de la piété filiale consiste à faire plaisir aux parents, et en même temps à ne pas contrarier leurs projets. Si l'on découvre des défauts dans l'agir des parents, on doit les avertir respectueusement. Confucius dit:

> Si vos parents tombent dans une faute, avertissez-les avec une grande douceur. Si vous les voyez déterminés à ne pas suivre vos avis, redoublez vos témoignages de respect, et réitérez vos remontrances. Quand même ils vous maltraiteraient, n'en ayez aucun ressentiment [21].

---

(19) Hio Eul; cf. Les quatre livres, p.73.
(20) Wei tcheng; cf. Les quatre livres, p.79.
(21) Li jenn; cf. Les quatre livres, p.105.

Lorsque des parents sont en faute, la renommée en est altérée. Les enfants ne peuvent pas rester indifférents. Ils doivent mettre leurs parents en garde avec une grande révérence, et si ceux-ci refusent de les écouter, les enfants doivent conserver à leur égard la même piété filiale. En effet, la piété confucéenne consiste avant tout à vénérer les parents. Meng tzue dit:

> Il y a trois choses que l'on considère partout comme respectables: la dignité, l'âge et la vertu. Ce qui obtient le plus de respect à la cour, c'est la dignité; dans les villages et les bourgs, c'est l'âge; en ceux qui travaillent à réformer les moeurs et dirigent le peuple, c'est la vertu [22].

Mais honorer les parents reste au-dessus de ces trois valeurs respectables. La piété filiale consommée est une vertu d'adulte, car elle demande un grand effort dans tous les domaines.

III. Comparaison Et Interpenetration

L'amour que Thérèse a pour Dieu, et la piété confucéenne pour les parents se basent tous les deux sur la "Vie". Thérèse aime Dieu, Source de la vie; les confucéens respectent leurs parents, car la vie vient d'eux. On aime Dieu pour toute la vie: on évite le mal qui déplaît à Dieu, on pratique le bien qui *honore* Dieu. De même on aime les parents comme le devoir de toute une vie: "toujours les honorer, ne jamais les peiner, veiller à les nourrir". La piété filiale confucéenne peut s'appliquer à Dieu, et même, en définitive, ne doit s'appliquer qu'à lui. Car la vie vient des parents, mais les parents sont aussi des hommes, et ils dépendent à leur tour de la Source de la vie. Ils ne peuvent être le but ultime de leurs enfants. Si on applique la piété filiale au service de Dieu, le principe "honorer les parents et ne jamais les peiner" peut correspondre avec la petite voie de Thérèse, et même avec la piété filiale de Jésus qui consiste à honorer le Père.

---

(22) Koung Suenn Tch'eou; cf. Les quatre livres, p.385.

Actuellement, la société chinoise évolue dans sa règle de vie comme dans sa morale et sa piété filiale traditionnelle, qui disparaissent peu à peu. Même si certains essayent de conserver ces valeurs, les enfants ne se considèrent plus comme le corps continu de leurs parents et éprouvent des difficultés à les servir de tout leur coeur. Cependant, si l'on pouvait élever la piété filiale confucéenne à un plus haut niveau (celui de Dieu:aimer et servir Dieu comme Source de la vie), non seulement on pourrait aider les chinois à comprendre facilement la relation entre l'homme et Dieu, mais de plus on pourrait contribuer à créer une spiritualité qui conviendrait parfaitement à la culture chinoise. Si cette nouvelle forme de piété filiale peut être harmonisée avec l'enfance spirituelle, ce serait une grande richesse, une lumière d'Extrême-Orient pour l'Eglise actuelle.

L'enfance spirituelle et la piété confucéenne se distinguent dans le fait que la première insiste sur l'amour tandis que la seconde exige le *respect*. L'amour peut produire l'égalité réciproque; le respect introduit une distance entre le supérieur et l'inférieur. Thérèse aime Dieu comme un enfant qui se trouve dans le bras d'un Père plein de tendresse. Par la grâce, le Père élève l'âme de Thérèse à la participation de la vie divine, à la ressemblamce; l'union devient possible. La piété filiale confucéenne considère les parents comme les supérieurs: il faut les aimer et les respecter. Le respect crée la distance. La civilité confucéenne insiste beaucoup sur ce point. Chou Hi dit:

> Chaque fois qu'ils le peuvent, les enfants doivent être au service de leurs parents, de leurs oncles ou de leurs tantes; ils doivent manifester une attitude toute respectueuse, agir avec beaucoup d'attention, parler avec déférence et à voix basse. Ils aident leurs parents à se lever ou à se mouvoir, ne se mouchent pas en leur présence, ni ne font aucun bruit. Ils ne s'assoient ou se retirent qu'après y avoir été invités. [23]

---

(23) Le Rituel de Chou Hi.

Les Morales intérieures de Liki donne des règles encore plus sévères pour la vie à la maison, mais elles ne sont observées que par les familles princières; les paysans ont tous une vie très simple. Cependant tous gardent le respect envers les parents: c'est la grande règle. Les enfants occidentaux recherchent surtout l'intimité avec leurs parents, et les adultes se montrent très simples à leur égard. La caractéristique de Thérèse est de se présenter devant Dieu avec un coeur d'enfant. Elle ne veut pas grandir devant Dieu, mais rester toujours une enfant pour garder son intimité avec Dieu. En réalité, qu'est-ce qu'avoir soixante-dix ou quatre-vingts ans devant l'Eternel? Dieu n'est dans le temps, mais dans le présent; un jour, pour lui, est comme mille ans. Dans la tradition chinoise, nous aimons évoquer Lao-leitzeu qui voulut, à l'âge de soixante-dix ans, plaire à ses parents en dansant avec de beaux vêtements. Il serait bon que les personnes âgées cherchent à plaire à Dieu en l'aimant avec un coeur d'enfant. Que sont, devant Dieu, le savoir, la puissance, les oeuvres des adultes ou des personnes âgées? Dieu regarde le coeur, il apprécie tout simplement le coeur pur et sincère des enfants. Jésus dit:

Si vous ne retournez à l'état des enfants, vous n'entrerez pas dans le Royaume des Cieux [24].

Dans la doctrine confucéenne, le respect demande que les enfants imitent les grandes personnes, et même, que les jeunes aient une attitude d'adulte mûr. Qu'ils sachent respecter leurs parents, et par conséquent garder leurs distances. En réalité, les relations entre les petits enfants et leurs parents sont plus empreintes d'amour et d'intimité que de respect. C'est pourquoi les Chinois peuvent comprendre qu'on aime ses parents avec un coeur d'enfant.

Il existe cependant un point difficile de la culture chinoise: on parle de respect et non d'amour à l'égard du Ciel. Respecter le Ciel est, pour la Chine, un très ancien enseignement. De plus le culte à

---

(24) Mt 18,3.

l'égard du Ciel est strictement reservé a l'empereur. Il a le privilège d'accomplir le sacrifice qui s'effectue hors de la Cité impériale. Ce sacrifice est la plus somptueuse cérémonie de la cour. Mais avant de l'offrir, l'empereur doit se demander si le pays est en prospérité, le peuple en paix, et la volonté du Ciel respectée. Depuis la fondation de la République Chinoise, il n'existe plus d'empereur, ni par conséquent de culte envers le Ciel.

Si l'on demande aux Chinois de vivre une intimité d'enfant avec Dieu, ils en éprouvent un sentiment d'irrespect. Par exemple, en Occident, l'amour entre l'époux et l'épouse représente l'amour entre le Christ et les fidèles. Les Chinois ne peuvent l'accepter car ils voient là une insulte à l'egard du Christ. Mais les Chinois peuvent envisager une piété filiale envers Dieu. Actuellement les familles, ainsi que la société chinoise, perdent graduellement le respect traditionnel envers les parents; elles commencent à imiter les Occidentaux en vivant d'intimité. Ainsi la pyschologie traditionnelle des Chinois évolue peu à peu, et l'amour envers Dieu pourra etre accepté, cependant toujours avec respect.

Après son ordination sacerdotale à l'Abbaye Sanit-André de Bruges, Don Lou n'osait pas célébrer la messe quotidiennement. En effet il avait longtemps été ambassadeur et ministre, et chaque fois qu'il devait être recu en audience par les rois, il tremblait à la perspective de manquer de respect. La messe étant le culte envers Dieu, sa crainte s'en trouva d'autant plus augmentée. Des amis lui expliquèrent qu'on célèbre la messe *in persona Christi*; le Christ est le Fils de Dieu, c'est donc en qualité de Fils que l'on célèbre la messe. Il ne faut pas avoir peur! Depuis lors, Don Lou eut le courage de monter à l'autel. En effet nous ne faisons qu'un Corps avec le Christ; en lui, nous devenons des fils adoptifs. Nous devons aimer le Père en faisant nôtres les sentiments du Christ lui-même. Il nous est alors possible d'approcher Dieu sans commettre de sacrilège.

Alors que la science se développe, et que le matérialisme touche à son apogée, le coeur humain éprouve un sentiment de vide et de sécheresse. Après deux guerres mondiales, devant la terreur et la haine engendrées par le nazisme et le communisme, le monde crie sa soif de respect mutuel et d'humanité. L'amour que Thérèse éprouve envers Dieu avec son coeur d'enfant est le meilleur remède pour l'Eglise d'aujourd'hui. L'enfance spirituelle permet aux hommes de notre temps de s'elancer vers le Père; ils expérimenteront alors au coeur une immense chaleur. Et nous, Chinois, qui avons vécu quatre-vingts ans de guerre civile, le conflit sino-japonais, la persécution communiste, levons les yeux vers le Ciel et, avec un coeur d'enfant, crions vers le Père. Shi-Ki dit:

> Le Ciel est le commencement des hommes; les parents sont leur fondement. Aussi quand l'homme se trouve dans une extrême pauvreté, il aspire à rentrer dans la maison paternelle; s'il éprouve un épuisement total, il ne peut s'empêcher de crier vers le Ciel. S'il est accablé de maladies, il appelle instinctivement ses parents.

Aimons donc le Père avec un coeur d'enfant. Alors, notre esprit trouvera un appui, notre vie son but, notre coeur la paix.

Philosophy of Life And
The Development of Chinese Philosophy

I.

The first edition of *Sheng-ming che-hsueh* [Philosophy of Life] was published in 1984. At the end of its preface, I wrote.

Can philosophy of life represent a reform of traditional Chinese philosophy and thus become China's new philosophy? Can philosophy of life, as a fusion of Catholic thought and Confucianism, serve as the foundation for the Church's acculturation? I invite the good-hearted reader to answer these questions. What I have done was only to express my own philosophical idea.

Four years later, I revised the first edition, which was subsequently published as the *Sheng-ming che-hsueh hsiu-ting pen* [Philosophy of Life, Revised Edition.] In its preface, I wrote.

I published *Sheng-ming che-hsueh* [Philosophy of Life] in 1984. Half of the book was written while I was confined at the Country Hospital. At that time, I tried to use the concept of "life" to establish a link between Chinese philosophy and Scholasticism, with stress on "interlinking". This made it necessary to present the important points of Chinese philosophy and Scholasticism in the book whose order of presentation followed traditional Scholastic philosophy. It gives the impression of a lecture on Scholasticism. Within a period of five years after its publication, I went deeper into the significance of philosophy of life, which resulted in the gradual formation of new ideas. Western philosophy deals with "being". A "being" is an object, or can be said to be "*ens*". But why is being a being? Western philosophy believes that what a being actually is needs no discussion. In fact, it cannot be discussed. In contrast, Chinese philosophy explains what being is. In Chinese philosophy, being is change. Why is being a being? It is because of "existence". What is "existence"? Existence is change. What is "change"? Changes is *sheng-sheng* [perpetual generation]. In Chinese philosophy, this "perpetual generation" is "life", although it does not explain what life is. I explained that life is an immanent process from "potency to act". I also explained "ens" as the "existent". Being results from existence. In turn, existence is continuous change. Because this continuous change is actualized inside the body, therefore it is life.

The revised edition of *Philosophy of Life* stresses the explanation of the concept of change using Scholoastic philosophical ideas by proceeding from potency to act. Changes in the substance are later studied to explain "life". I also explained the role played by philosophy of life in Chinese philosophy over the centuries. Two years after the publication of the revised edition, I published the final edition of the book in 1990. This edition represents the formal representative work of my philosophical thinking, in a way showing that my philosophical ideas have finally attained a final form and that systematization of my ideas have eventually been completed. The final edition includes an additional chapter on "Creation", which explains the origin of the universe and in which I explained the idea of "generative force" in great detail. Two years later, I published in 1993, a sequel of *Philosophy of Life* in which a few important issues on philosophy of life were discussed with more depth. Among these issues include the concept of "reality" (substance), Epistemology, and the relationship between truth, goodness and beauty with history and life. In these explanations, I intended to interlink "life" with all aspects of philosophy on the metaphysical and ontological levels. Despite all these, I still intend to write and publish another sequel on philosophy of life centering on the many issues related to ontology and epistemology.

II.

After integrating the final edition and the sequel of the *Philosophy of Life*, philosophy of life can be described as follows:

Philosophy of life starts with the concept of "motion". Western metaphysical ontology discusses "being" as the highest rationalization of the universe and all things. In the final analysis, the universe and all things are but "being". In Greek philosophy and early Scholastic philosophy, "being" is taken as a "reality" (substance), with "being" and "existence" inseparably united. However, after th Middle Ages, "being" and "existence" became separated conceptually. "Being" became a universal concept. It only includes the concept of "nature" and does not embrace the concept of "existence". Only the Absolute Being is a "being" that includes the concept of "existence". The universe and all things do not conceptaully include "existence". "Being" is explained through the concept of "nature", not thorugh "existence". As a result, all targets of philosophical studies were explained in terms of "nature". For instance, reality, accidents, and so on were all defined by explaining what they are. At the same time, this also led to a principle: philosophy studies universal concepts, not acutal individual things. Thus, metaphysics became a study of abstract concepts, although these concepts have their actual basis in concrete individual things.

The *I Ching* [Book of Changes] studies the universe and myriad thing. It equates the myriad things with the myriad beings. For it, things are concrete, not abstract concepts. The *I Ching* explains the universe and the myriad things from the perspective of "existence". It does not discuss what the myriad things are in defining the latter. Instead, it explains what actual, concrete things are by pointing out that they are action. That is to say, the "existence" of the universe and the myriad things are mobile, and, in fact, changing. The *I Ching* explains changes, specifically, the changes occurring in the universe and all myriad things.

Changes occurring in the universe and all myriad things come about due to the union of *yin* and *yang* elements. In the *I Ching, yin* and *yang* are represented by ch'ien [heaven] and *k'un* [earth]. Both *yin* and *yang* are elements of *ch'i* [material force]. They possess different characteristics. *Yang* is powerful while *yin* is mild in nature. Whereas *yang* is tough, *yin* is submissive. *Yin* and *yang* fuse to form the *wu-hsing* [Five Agents] which consist of metal, wood, water, fire and earth. In turn, the Five Agents fuse to form things. The Five Agents continuously act in the universe, fusing together to generate the myriad things. The *I Ching* says: "Change is the perpetual generation of life." Changes occurring among *yin* and *yang* and the Five Agents generate the myriad things without end, thus making the universe a "flood of life".

Within the generated myriad things, *yin* and *yang* and the Five Agents continue changing. Confucianists call this continuous immanent change "life". For them, all the myriad things have life. The lives of the universe and of all the myriad things interlink with one another, in this way forming one life. Wang Yang-ming called this "the unity of benevolence [*jen*]." Chang Tsai described this as "Heaven is the father and earth is the mother... I and others are brothers. Things and me join together" (*Hsi Ming* [Western Inscription]). Chu Hsi explained the idea of one life as man's attainment of the mind of Heaven and earth. Since Heaven and earth have their mind in the generation of things, then man's mind is benevolent. Benevolence and generation are itterlinked. Heaven and earth represent *yin* and *yang*, *ch'ien* and *k'un*. Then all changes are for the generation of life. Thus, man's whole life is itself "benevolence". Benevolence is the foundation of all virtues. Confucianists thus equate the exercise of filial piety with benevolence. The Confucianist concept of filial piety finds its basis in life.

From all these, we can see that Confucianism is a philosophy of life.

III.

The Confucianist philosophy of life has received the confirmation of contemporary neo-Confucianists such as Thome Fang, Tang Chun-yi, Liang Su-ming and Mou Tsung-san who all emphasized that Confucian philosophy is centered on life. In spite of this, however, nobody continued explaining this issue, much less developed it. I used ideas inherent to Scholastic philosophy in developing the Confucianist philosophy of life. I have established a metaphysical system for philosophy of life, and eventually set a foundation for spiritual life.

Confucianist discussion of the universe and myriad things starts from the *I Chings* definition of *ch'ien* [heaven] as "the origin of all origins" and of *k'un* [earth] as "the reason for the generation of myriad things." Both heaven and earth are described as origins. The *I Ch'uan* also says: "Change possesses the Great Ultimate, which, in turn, generated *yin and yang*" Chou Tun-i's Diagram of the Great Ultimate equates the Great Ultimate with the Non-ultimate, which generates *yin* and *yang*. *Yin* and *yang* lead to the Five Agents, which, in turn, beget male and female. Male and female generate the myriad things. These ideas only describe the process of generation. They do not discuss its origins. This is because the *I Ching* and the Idealists do not consider the Great Ultimate as self-existing. Both the *Book of History* and the *Book of Odes* mention the idea of a god who created the myriad things. Similarly, Confucianist tradition also includes the idea of a "lord of creation" or "creator".

Thus, my philosophy of life confirms that the universe was created by God. God used his supernatural power in creating the universe, the latter not derived nor emanating from his substance, but instead, through power. This supernatural power is called the creative power. Creative power created the universe, an immense energy or motive force called generative power. Contemporary physicists and astronomers take the universe as an immense motive force in constant action. The matter of generative power is material. That is, the material of the universe was created by the creative power of God *ex nihilo*. An immense blackness at the very start, the universe did not have a fixed configuration. Chapter I of the Old Testament's Genesis says: "In the beginning God created the heavens and the earth. Now the earth was a formless void, there was darkness over the deep...." In Chapter XII of this *Confessoins* St. Augustine wrote that at the beginning, heaven and earth were a mass of indeterminate matter that appeared utterly black. Contemporary astronomy also describes the primeval universe as a violently moving mass of gas that later exploded and formed the stars and the galaxies. Lao-tzu once said that "Tao" is nebulous and formless. Chang Tasi described the "Great Harmony" as "as ascending, descending and moving in all ways without ceasing, the start of all interaction, extension and contraction." The universe was originally a mass of formless matter that possessed tremendous motive force. Its matter was created by God out of nothing. The *li* (form) of the universe was God's "idea" in creating the universe. The universe's power is derived from God's creative power. The universe created by God is an active, ever-changing universe.

The motive force of the universe is called generative power, which is derived from God's creative power. Generative power consists of two mutually acting motive forces known to ancient Chinese philosopers as *yin* and *yang* . These two motive forces are constantly in action, joining together to generate the myriad things. While in action, the two motive forces of the generative power fuse together when conditions are appropriate, resulting in the generation of things suited for these conditions. The matter of the thing generated is the same matter of the universe while its form is God's idea in creating it. This idea is transferred from creative power to generative power whose two motive force fuse to generate something based on this form. With respect to God, creative power is beyond time. With respect to the universe, creative power is everlasting. Its generation of things through generative power is what St. Thomas called "continuous creation."

After their generation, things' "existence" is a moving existence. This existence moves and changes, and, is therefore, change. Since things are generated through generative power, they also possess its two motive forces. The two motive forces continue moving within the thing. Wang Ch'uan -shan thus once said: "Life decreases while nature increases day-by-day." Confucianists thus propose that all things possess life.

Life is the immanent action of things. Within things in the universe, motions of life constantly generate change. Thus life is change. Not only do animals and plants are constantly changing, minerals also undergo change. Change is the process from potency to act. Scholastic philosophy only recognizes accidental change. When substances change, it is a process of annihilation. In philosophy of life, the immanently moving life undergoes substantial change wherein the two motive forces of generative power act through the potency of already formed realities. This is analogous to parents begtting offspring. The two motive forces of the generative power emanate from the potency of the parents' substances, begetting sons and daughters. After the birth of the offspring, the substance's motive forces again use its potency to "again move and fuse to form a new thing. Since the form of the new thing does not change, its nature does not change either. It remains the thing with the same nature." Wang Ch'uan-shan's "Life decreases while nature increases day-by-day" means that *yin* and *yang* operate continuously within things, fusing and generating things' nature. This nature is determined by the Mandate of Heaven. Although a thing's Mandate of Heaven constantly decreases, it remains the same Mandate of Heaven. *Yin* and *yang* remain unchanged following the nature determined by the Mandate of Heaven. Philosophy of life propounds that a thing's form is transmitted from creative power to generative power, which generates the thing's nature based on this form. The two forces of the generative power constantly change within a thing. The form is constantly the same form transmitted to the generative power from creative power. For instance, my life constantly changes. The form of this change is the idea of God in creating me. This idea is called Mandate of Heaven. God's idea of creating me is constantly transmitted to my immanent generative power by creative power. The immanent changes effected in my by generative power constantly follows this "form". As a result, I remain I. We ordinarily say that our lives are ever-changing. However, our life moves on following God's holy will.

Philosophy of life takes changes in life as accidental changes. My substance remains unchanged. What undergoes change are my accident, that is, the changes are physical quantitative change or spiritual qualitative change. However, changes in my body are changes in the integral reality. The so-called accidents are also elements belonging to me. Without these elements, I would cease to exist. In Chinese philosophy, the elements of the "ego" depend upon the darity or turbidity of *ch'i* (materia force) and the Five Agents. They make up the components of the substance. Life extends throughout all the parts of a person. Therefore, changes in life are changes occurring in the whole person.

IV.

Each thing is an integral reality. In Scholastic philosophy, realities are made up of substance and accidents. Substance and accidents join to form an individual. Ordinarily, Scholastic philosophy refers to substance as reality. Any change in the reality is accidental change.

Philosophy of life takes a reality as an integral that includes substance and accidents. Man is psychophysical, with his soul forming part of his substance. Similarly, his body also forms part of his substance. "Ego" is an individual, including all that it possesses, such as the size and color of its body, and its mind's intellect and emotions. Because all these make up the components of the "ego", the absence of one renders the "ego" incomplete. Life is the "existence" of the "ego" -- an integral reality. It is the movement of the integral reality. Life is the factor that makes the integral reality "one". "Ego" is because it exists. "Ego" exists because it lives. As long as the "ego" lives, it remains always is. If "ego" does not live, its body and soul separate. Its extremities and bodily organs also decay and disintegrate.

Substance and accidents are two concepts that can be differentiated and taken separately. Actually, all things in the universe are made up of substance and accidents. They join together because of actual existence. Actual existence is life. The "ego's" body and soul unite because of life. Similarly, all the parts of a body join together owing to life. If Paralysis strikes a certain part of the body, it loses life, upon which this part becomes dissociated from the entire body. In theory, substance and accidents can be separated. In actual terms, however, they are inseparable.

Contemporary physics explains matter in terms of energy, equating these two concepts with one another. Matter is made up of moving energy. Matter is traditonally explained as being composed of material elements. Now, matter is explained as being made up of moving energy. Matter is differentiated by quantities of moving energy. In philosophy of life, all things are moving things. They are themselves generative power. Generative power has its own matter, or else it would become empty and would not exist. Actually, motion and energy in modern physics must also possess matter. Since each thing is immanent action, then immanent action is itself "existence". Not only do plants and animals become actual, individual realities because of immanent action--life, minerals also become individuals because of immanent action. In Scholastic philosophy, individual minerals are but made up of quantity or space arising out of their "form". Each mineral or artifical object possesses its own form. However, exterior form cannot cause an internal fusion of material components. This is because the destruction of minerals or artifical objects does not result from its external form, but rather, is due to a disintegration of its components. The fusion or disintegration of components comes about through internal moving energy. If due to external pressure, internal moving energy is prevented from continuous motion, the object suffers damage. For instance, exposure to the elements destroys a rock.

For a reality to be known, it itself must be bright. This brightness differs owing to characteristics of things. Pure spiritual beings are naturally bright in their totality. In contrast, material realities are bright owing to their substance. In order to know, man uses his mind to utilize his bodily functions. Man cannot directly know purely spiritual beings. He cannot use the so-called intuition. Instead, he uses the sense organs to know objective functions. He uses his intellect to know the function known by sense organs, which help him infer the substance of the function. In Chinese philosophy, reality and function and undifferentiated. In terms of substance, reality and function are differentiated. In epistemology, however, reality and function are one.

For one to know a reality, he must know reality in its totality, including its substance and accidents. Ordinarily, we say that philosophy deals with principles, not individual things. Dealing with principles means talking about concepts, abstraction and metaphysics. Yet, the universe and all things are actual individuals. Sepearating concepts with realities results in many interpretations of concepts. In fact, it is enough to create other Chinese schools of thought.

V.

Man's life, higher than the lives of all things in the universe, is a life consisting of the union of body and soul. Life continues to develop without end in a process Chinese philosophers called "fulfillment of nature". A psychophysical life, although possessing spiritual and physical balance that avoids partiality, is mainly spiritual in the sense that the soul directs the body. In Chinese philosophy, the development of life requires an understanding of the wonders of life and the completion of all its processes. Life is a union. The universe and life are one. The principle of the universe and of life rests on the Tao of Heaven whose purpose it is to generate all things. Therefore, man must unite his virtues with those of heaven.

Philosophy of life views the universe and life as one and interlinked. The development of man's life starts with his family. As Mencius said: "Love you next of kin." Then, it develops toward society whereupon one treats other people as one would oneself, and whereupon one "respects other people's elder and property as one would with his own." Mencius called this "benevolence to others." Then, man's life must extend towards the universe and all things by caring for all things, using things in the nature world in a reasonable way, and avoiding abuse in the process. This Mencius called "love of things." The lives of things in the universe are interlinked. Destroy a type of living thing and other types also get harmed, which eventually endangers man's life. This is the reason behind the importance of environmental issues.

In "the union of the virtues of heaven and man", "heaven" does not refer to the blue sky. Instead, it refers to the "Heaven" that created the world. Heaven and earth are the function (*yung*) of Heaven. They represent the action of Heaven. Man's life must unite with the love of Heaven. Heaven or God is an absolute spirit. Since man's soul is also spiritual, he can use his soul to unite with the love of God. If man develops spiritual love and aspires for the purely spiritual God, and in so doing, transcends material things in such a way that he does not covet material things or get attached to earthly affairs, then he enjoys spiritual peace and becomes able to enter everlasting life after death.

Viewed from the angle of Chinese philosophy, philosophy of life can be the way to develop the former. This is because traditional Chinese philosophy is a philosophy that deals with life. Both Confucianism and Taoism show such as tradition. Furthermore, life is the very foundation of Chinese philosophy, as well as its special point. We must therefore continue developing it. This philosophy that develops the concept of life matches contemporary Western philosophical trends. Contemporary Western philosophy starts from the abstract concept of "being" and proceeds to the concrete idea of "existence". It proceeds from a static cosmology towards a mobile one, as in the new trends in the philosophies of Bergson, Whitehead and the Existentialists. In today's West, there is now the so-called "Theory of Metaphysical Experience" and "Human Hermeneutics", both of which take individual life as the meaning of the "ego". Historicism and Moral Relativism, although less accurate, are also founded on life. Our discussion of philosophy of life finds its basis on the metaphysics of life. It is in no way a special isolated philosophical thought. Instead, philosophy of life fuses traditional Chinese philosophy with its traditional Western counterpart in the search toward development.

Ching-Hsing（盡性）
(Fulfillment of Nature)
in the
Doctrine of the Mean（中庸）

The central tenet of the *Doctrine of the Mean* can be summarized in a word: Nature, which is understood in terms both of physical and human nature. Thus it is necessary to have a clear view of nature. Nature comes originally and directly from the Mandate of Heaven which consists of two essential characteristics: naturalness and innateness. This work will not seek simply to explain their meaning, but will look for their genesis, especially from a philosophical perspective.

I. The Origin of The Natural and The Innate

The very first question is, how this naturalness and innateness come to be? A simple explanation of these phenomena will not provide a satisfactory answer. We must instead trace their gensis back to the Mandate of Heaven (Heaven-Mandate) which is shared commonly in the Chinese tradition. Mencius for example used both terms in the same context:

> It is due to our nature that our mouths desire sweet tastes, that our eyes desire beautiful colors, that our ears desire pleasant sounds, that our noses desire fragrant odors and that our four limbs desire ease and comfort. But there is also fate. The superior man does not say they are man's nature. The virtue of humanity in the relationship between father and son, the virtue of righteousness in the relationship between ruler and ministers, the virtue of propriety between guest and host, the virtue of wisdom in the worthy, and the sage in regard to the Way of Heaven--these are endowed in pepole in various degrees

according to fate. But there is also man's nature. The superior
man does not refrain from practicing them and say they are the
matters of fate. [1]

In the *Book of History* and the *Annalects* the terms of Heaven-
Mandate and Fate clearly express the fate determined Heaven or *T'ien*.
But to be more precise, these two terms are not identical. Though
Mencius himself uses these two terms in the same sense, still he
acknowledges their difference in their very original meaning. He has
in his mind two different conceptions: the small substance (hsiao-ti)
which is concerned with physical elements and the great substance (ta-
ti) which deals with the human heart and mind. The small substance is
completely determined or created, and it belongs to the category of
fate, while the great substance belongs to what we call human nature
and can win over blind fate.

Accordingly, human morals have been constructed on human
nature, i.e., the human hear, and mind. Mencius regards morals in
different forms such as benevolence (Jen), righteousness (Yi), fittingness (Li) and wisdom (Chi):

> What belongs by his nature to the superior man are benevo-
> lence, reighteousness, propriety and wisdom.... These are
> rooted in his heart; their growth and manifestation are mild
> harmony appearing in the countenance or rich fullness in the
> back, and the character imparted to the four limbs. Those limbs
> understand to arrange themselves without being told. [2]

In the *Doctrine of the Mean*, human nature is known not by its
essence, but by its praxis (or acts manifest in nature). But this distinction does not contradict the view that they all belong to human nature.
A careful study of the history of metaphysics leads to the same conclu-

---

(1) *Mencius*, Ching-Hsin, passage 1, Chan Wing-tsit, *A Source Book in Chinese
    Philosophy*, pp. 81-82.
(2) Ching-hsin, 2; James Legge, vol. 2, p. 460.

sion. For example, Western metaphysics seems to put more emphasis on the question of Being (in its essence) while the Chinese counterpart tends toward a metaphysics of natural change. Such distinction is artificial, because praxis and theory, existence and essence, change and being cannot be discarded. Only by means of act (change) does Being come into its presence (sheng). That is to say, in its most original form, the act of coming into presence (sheng), i.e. existence, requires a movement beforehand. In another expression, the nature of our existence is dynamic presence. Analogously, one could also say that the nature of Being could be seen from its immobility or its essence. In the *Doctrine of the Mean* man's nature is precisely understood in this dynamic perspective.

Movement, change, dynamos... all express *living* human life. Any discussion about human nature is indentified with a discussion about our life. Hence, it can also be said that we can understand our life only if we first grasp our human nature. It is no wonder then that for Confucius and Mencius, all moral codes which are purposely constructed to regulate our life must be built on the basis of human nature. The following passage in the *Doctrine of the Mean* clearly indicates that: "The Ordinance of Heaven is what we call the law of nature. To fulfill the law of nature is what we call the way. To cultivate the way is what we call education" (Chap. 1).

Accordingly, living in accordance with human nature is called Cheng or sincerity. In the *Book of the Great Learning* this is exalted as the most pristine virtue. In this way, all morals are constructed upon human nature as goodness itself, i.e., the basic virtue. Thus, we can state that human nature is not only goodness itself, on which all morals are based, but is *most evident* which needs no clarification or verification. A neo-confucianist, Wang Yang-ming calls it moral conscience (liang-chih). Moral conscience is innate, a *priori* in the sense of what Mencius discribes as ' unlearned knowledge' or knowledge acquired not from learning, or innate idea; the foundation of morals, moral conscience must be the common consciousness of all men: an unconscious moral conscience would be rather a non-sense. However, that does not mean that all men are equally good. Man often lapses into ignorance for one or another reason, which is precisely why man needs self-enlightenment in order to restore moral conscience. This self-restoring enlightenment is expressed in the *Great Learning* as ' Let the virtue be self manifesting' or ' refurbishing pristine virtue', and in the *Doctrine of the Mean* as sincerity (Chap. 20): "Sincerity is the Way of Heaven. The attainment of sincerity is the way of men". [3]

On the other hand, there is also what we call physical or biological nature implicit in matter and which man needs to transform or to harmonize into goodness. By means of his own effort man can attain or acquire the goodness for his life. With a full knowledge of human nature man no longer clings to self-interest but voluntarily follows the natural way and as such becomes *Chun-tzu or* the noble man. In the *Doctrine of the Mean*, there is a passage:

> Sincerity in its original enlightened state is called nature; when manifested, it is called education. Where there is sincerity, there is manifestation; where there is manifestation. there is sincerity (Chap. 21).

Seen in this way, in its ' very nature' sincerity is transparent and spontaneous. Blinded by the strong desire to amass interests, man is in need of self--correction in order simple to return to his nature. Such is the purpose of education.

Regarding the question of nature, we find in the *Doctrine of the Mean* three main ideas: 1. human nature as Heaven-Mandtae, 2. human nature as goodness, and 3. human nature as the moral codes of human life. In a word, one can obtain the Tao only by means of educating one's human nature.

II. Sincerity

To attain the Tao, sincerity is the first requisite. The second half of the *Doctrine of the Mean* is devoted to this question of sincerity,

---

(3) Legge, vol. 2., p.413.

Cheng. This is implicit in all human activites guiding our praxis into conformity to human nature. Human nature may be regarded as the model or the standard with which man must act in accord. We regard it as the standard because of its universality and necessity. Another function of sincerity is its role in making nature moving and transforming:

> Where there is sincerity, there is form. Where there is form, there is evidence. Where there is evidence, there is manifestation. Where there is manifestation, there is activity. Where there is activity, there is change. Where there is change, there is transformation. In the world, only he who possesses sincerity can transform (Chap. 23).

In commenting on this passage, Chu-Hsi notes on the concepts of change and transformation as follows: change is always oriented toward *Chi* (the material force), and transformation toward the divinity. Thus he explains the difference of the attitude of a sage from that of ordinary people: "Only the mover can move all things and only the transformer can transform" (Chu-Hsi). However, if we take a careful look into the *Doctrine of the Mean*, it is clear that we cannot rely on the influence of the ordinary man to explain change and transformation. We can do that only by means of first grasping human nature (Chap. 22) and, more important, the "silent dynamic nature" (Ching Hsing). Consequently, our activities should be regulated by the morals based on human nature. By doing so, one can reach the stage of the sage. Needless to say, goodness is born in and from our sincerity and from our acts conforming to nature. Conversely, one can say also that our nature is in developing through moral acts. In the *Doctrine of the Mean*, goodness is identified with moral goodness:

> When the passions, such as joy, anger, grief and pleasure, have not awaken, that is our true self or being. When these passions awaken and each and all attain due measure and degree, that is the moral order (Chap. 3,4).

One important thing hidden in this passage that we need to mention is the key-term "harmony". Harmony expresses how human beings whenever and wherever -- in any state of joy, anger, sorrow and happiness --always try to act in accordance with the laws of nature. In a word, goodness means exactly the final stage of acting and developing as well as of following nature.

One point however, needs to be clarified here. In the *Doctrine of the Mean*, hsing, i.e. nature, can be understood not from its static appearance, but from is dynamic hidden aspect. That is to say, by means of a constant developing sincerity human nature manifests itself. In *I-King*, we find such an idea: ' Only through *yin* and *yang* does Tao manifest itself; only through practical acts does goodness reveal itself and only in sincerity does human nature emerge' (*I-King*, Chap. 5). In another expression, the autonomous transformation of *yin* and *yang* produces the nature of material and physical nature, and even these continue to further this self-transformation. Mencius thus regards human nature as goodness; as such, man has no other choice but out of sincerity to conserve and develop his nature. But to develop one's nature, one cannot look elsewhere for other ways; one must develop one's own nature in the natural way. Mencius explains:

> There are few in the world who can resist the temptation of helping their rice plants grow. Some leave them unattended, because they think that to help the plants is all to no avail; there are people who do not even bother to weed. Others help the plants grow by pulling at them; not only do they fail to help but they do harm. [4]

We can state it this way: like a seed which grows, human nature also consists in growing. Mencius means by seed what he has in his mind: benevolence, righteousness, fittingness and wisdom. These four cardianl virtues from the kernel of morality, namely goodness. One can say that these four virtues are regarded by Mencius not only as moral goodness but, more than that, the spiritual life itself, because spiritual life is meant for humankind. It is the great substance (ta-ti).

---

(4) *Mencius*, Kung-sun, 1.

However, in order to make them visible one should cultivate one's life. The moral act, i.e., the act of benevolence, righteousness, fittingness and wisdom, is rooted deeply in our spiritual life, or more precisely, in our human nature.

To avoid misunderstanding, we need to note here the difference between Western and Chinese metaphysics on this question. The Western metaphysicians discuss Being in terms of the principles of identity and of contradiction, while their Chinese counterparts understand being in its act of coming-into-presence in terms of moral virtues, i.e. the four cardinal virtues.

Let us return to Mencius's arguments. Our nature grows in the same way as a seed which, after being buried under the earth, grows up and again is planted in the rice-pad. The seed will become what it is supposed to be. According to this natural phenomenon, one may assert that the nature of a seed is to be such, i.e. following the principle implicit in the seed enables the seed itself to grow. The harvest self-expresses the total reason of this principle of *"sheng"* (genesis, creation....) Similarly, the principle implicit in nature can be explained in what I propose to call "ching-hsing", or the "silent, dynamic nature".

In the Doctrine of the Mean human nature must be understood as this "silent dynamic nature". At the very first beginning of human life, one notices the presence of a certain principle implicit in man (that we call *li*). Such a principle is known in the acts of benevolence, rightousness, fittingness and wisdom. Accepting *li* as the root requires that we develop our human nature by means of moral practice to the requirement of li. *Li is most visible in the life of Chun-tzu, the holy man or sage, who posses*ses these cardinal virtues:

> In the world, only he who possesses pervasive sincerity is able to fulfill his nature completely. He who is able to fulfill his own nature completely will be able to fulfill completely the nature of all men. He who is able to fulfill completely the nature of all men will be able to fulfill completely the nature of

all things. He who is able to fulfill completely the nature of all things will be able to assist the transforming and nourishing powers of Heaven and Earth. Able to assist the transforming and nourishing powers of Heaven and Earth, he may form a trinity with them (Chap. XXII).

The silent dynamic nature is the *Doctrine of the Mean* is manifested in four degrees: dynamic individuality, dynamic human nature, dynamic material force and dynamic transformation. These four degrees or steps are sometimes placed in time-sequence and sometimes occur at the same time. Generally speaking, in order to attain the fullness of human nature, it is necessary to proceed in order step by step, from the first to the second, from the second to the third and so on to the final step. A clarification about the time-sequence must be made here: at the very moment of reaching the first step, one reaches all four steps at one glace. Chu Hsi tends to a second interpretation, namely, claiming that one becomes a sage when he possesses sincerity (Chu Hsi).

In fact, the comment of Chu-Hsi is derived from his understanding of traditional morality based on Tao, and of the relationship between sincerity and human nature. Consequently, he claims that one can grasp completely one's own nature as well as the nature of universe, and that man should rely only on his nature as guide to acting. Chu-Hsi accepts the silent dynamic nature in the *Doctrine of the Mean* as a metaphysical essence in which one develops human nature to its most perfect form.

Following this interpretation, Wang Pan-shan continues to insist that the more the nature grows the more fate diminishes, because human nature is constructed on the unity of *yin* and *yang*. *Yin-yang* moves, transforms and constructs everything; it explains how human nature manifests itself. In this context, man and thing originally share the same nature: all depend on the Heaven-Mandate which is unchanging. Thus we can understand why the *Doctrine of the Mean* explains *hsing* (nature) and *li* (principle) in different terms. This idea strengthens our interpretation that the principle of Heaven-Mandate is unchangeable while our human nature is developing. Chu-Hsi has distinguished the principle (li) from material force *(chi)*. He argues that if nature is principle then this principle is unchangeable. But by taking nature as *chi* (material force), nature is seen to consist in developing. In the same sense, he baptized as individual nature the characteristics of each individual man. By taking *chi* as the most fundamental principle of nature, he claims that one attains the full knowledge of goodness and evil, i.e., one develops himself. Thus, this principle also is called the eternal principle of Heaven and Earth. However, Chu-Hsi notes that the nature of *chi* and of the Heaven and Earth are different in terms of manifestation. The nature of Heaven and Earth is abstract while that of *chi* is concrete.

In the *Doctrine of the Mean* we find both the concrete and abstract natures. To be more precise, note the main features of nature: the first is individual, the second is concrete nature, while the third concerns the nature of matter. Needless to say, the *Doctrine of the Mean tends* toward the second, concrete nature. In a word, we believe that Chinese metaphysics starts not from pure being but being in its concrete life and development. We would go a step further to say that it is through the movement of life (life in act) and by means of the concreteness of life that we can understand human nature. The evidence in our life: human growth from infancy to adulthood, from adulthood to the final stage of life, suggests continuous development. But how explain the diminution of human physical strength in old age? In fact we are talking of development in terms of spiritual development. The human spirit always develops, even at the later stage of our life, and to such a degree that one can obtain then the state of silent dynamic nature and become the sage.

III. Human Nature and The Nature of Thing

The last question regarding the silent dynamic nature in the *Doctrine of the Mean* is the nature of thing which, as Chu-Hsi insists, can be seen in our human nature. As a matter of fact, some explanations of human nature and the nature of thing have been made in terms of individual nature. But the reality is that whatever we name, either individual nature or human nature, either the nature of thing or simple nature, all belong to the same unique nature. A danger may occur in such an understanding of nature, namely, one may idenify human nature with animal nature, whereas the simple fact that man is not a beast demonstrates that human nature is not animal nature. In order to avoid this embarrassing problem, Chu-Hsi takes the view of Changtsai and Chang-chin on *li*. This explains all things in Heaven and Earth, but not on *chi* (material force) and on concrete *praxis* which are different in different species. [5]

Actually, Chu-Hsi holds that there are different stages of *chi*, from the innumerable to the seriousness, and from the seriousness (as the pshcyological prerequisite for true knowledge) to *chi*. On the other hand, he claims that the principle or *li* lies in actualizing, its degree of actualization depending on the seriousness of *chi*. More clearly, a man who possesses *chi* has the seriousness with which he knows how to let the self-manifesting take place. Chu-Hsi later reaffirms this position by reiterating that man can be understood from his total possession of the principle of all things *(li)*, while material things or animals can be grasped partly because they lack this *li*. In a word, the *li* found in the united and harmonious universe can be the principle of life, namely the principle of *sheng* or biological, genetic principle.

In *I-King*, similar ideas are found. Tao is the genetic activity which is implicit in the universe and expresses life. It contains in itself the movement of yin and yang. By taking *sheng* (genesis) as principle, or, more precisely, by taking life as principle, it is evident that the principle of life is identified with the principle of Heaven-Earth, that the most concrete principle must be the principle of *chi*, and finally, that the principle of life is in harmony with *chi* itself. From a reverse order, one may formulate it so: if *chi* stands in opposition to life, then the principle *(li)* will not become present, and logically, no life can be

---

(5) *Chu-Hsi Yu Lei*, Chap. 18 and Chap. 1.

expected. Hence, only by means of the seriousness of *chi* does life emerge. According to Chu-Hsi then the more the seriousness of *chi* develops, the more life ascends toward its most developed form, i.e., human life. One may say also, with man *chi* is in its highest seriousness and therefore life manifests itself in the most perfect form, namely, spiritual life whose essential characteristics are benevolence, righteousness, fittingness and wisdom. In Chu-Hsi's own words, that is the united principle in its manifestation.

However, in our daily life, the four cardinal virtues of benevolence, righteousness, fittingness and wisdom are often clouded by improper events. The duty of self control and correction is thus the first condition for arriving at the silent dynamic nature, and then attaining the full developing personality. A man's personality is known in spiritual life, which consists of human life, as well as in cosmic life. Thus, Mencius affirms: "All things are there in us" (Ching-hsing, 1). The silent, dynmaic nature, now regarded as the great ultimate force, involves both human nature and the nature of things. In *I-King*, this *hsing* or nature is considered as the principle of life coming from Heaven and Earth: "The Virtues of Heaven and Earth are implicit in *sheng* (genesis), i.e., our original life can be found in the love of the heavenly spirit" (T'ien Hsin). Similarly, Chu-Hsi insists on the spiritual force as the basis of Heaven and Earth. Once man possesses spiritual force, he is fully developed. [6] One can also express this as once man arrives at the stage of quietness of hear (and mind), he can express (from his life) the benevolence existing in Heaven and Earth. Mencius speaks thus of benevolence: "he is benevolent towards the people, but is merely sparing with things". [7] As such, one has all the virtues existing in the harmony of Heavey and Earth; as a logical matter one absolves himself from all conflicts in the universe. In the *Yi-chuan*, the same idea is expressed as follows: "A great man possesses the virtues implicit in Heaven and on Earth". [8]

---

(6) *The School of Chu-Hsi*, Chap. 17.

(7) Mencius, Chap. 45.

(8) I-Chuan, Hexagrams of Chien and Kwa.

To conclude, we cite from the *Doctrine of the Mean* a passage which expresses the above idea: "Oh, how great the Way of the sage is! Vast and full, it gives birth and life to all created things" (Chap. 27.1).

Metaphysical Issues is
The Philosophy of Life [1]

I. Generative Power

Metaphysics studies "being". When a being is existing, then it is a "reality." This "existence" does not belong to the abstract, theoretical realm, but rather, to the actual world. An actual existence is "act", or constant immanence, the act of living, or even, life itself.

God, the Absolute Being, is pure "Act." He is moving although unchanging, and yet he forms a "Trinity." The "Trinity" is absolutely pure life, simple and not complex, clear and resplendent.

God, the "Pure Act," created the universe with his omnipotent power. The universe he created is a limitless motive force derived from his omnipotent creative power. This limitless motive force is called generative power. The *chih* (matter) of generative power (or the universe) was created by the omnipotent creative power *ex nihilo*. The *li* (principle, form) of generative power (or the universe) is the Creator's idea in creating the universe. These matter and form were then fused together by generative power to form the one universe.

The universe is power *per se*. It is itself the generative power. Generative power consists of positive and negative powers, which mutually ebb and flow, a process which, in turn, leads to the genera-

---

(1) [Author's Note] In my book *Sheng-ming che-hsueh* [Philosophy of Life] and its sequel, I explained the metaphysical issues on Philosophy of Life. However, some of these issues still require further study. In this article, I dealt with these topics in a simple and systematic way. A more detailed and more comprehensive explanation will be presented in a book I intend to write in the near future.

tive power's (or the universe's) continuous "act." The universe's "act" creates changes, which generate the myriad things. As the *I Ching* says: " *I* (Chang) is the perpetual generation of life" (Appended Remarks, Part 1, Chapter V).

By the "act" of the generative power (universe), each thing exists after the union of cosmic matter with the Creator's idea of that thing arising from the generative power, by virtue of the creative power. Things of the universe are teeming with life and are in perpetual generation, which leads to new things. This process manifests an evolutionary phenomenon, the very same phenomenon St. Augustine and St. Thomas Aquinas referred to as "continual creation." In terms of God, the creation of the universe manifested the fact that the creative action is beyond time. In terms of the universe, it meant continuous changes, which suggest a process happening within time. The universe's continuous changes cannot happen without God's creative power. The generation of each thing is in itself one process of creation. The matter of things comes from cosmic matter while the form of things is God's idea of creating those things. In ancient Chinese philosophy, the latter is called *ming* (fate), or *T'ien-ming* (Mandate of Heaven). It is bestowed to the generative power through creative power, after which it leads to the generation of something. The generation of all things in the universe follows some kind of evolutionary batches. In this process, the basis of evolution is a change in the environment. "Survival of the fittest" is, in fact, one principle of evolution. The corporeal principle of new things, in contrast, is dervied from God's idea of creating these things. Wang Ch'uan-shan once said: "Life decreases while nature increases day by day." Every person's soul (principle, primal form) directly comes from God. By virtue of creative power, it is bestowed with generative power, which, in turn, unites body and soul together.

In ancient Chinese philosophy, nature *(hsing)* is taken as principle *(li)*. *Li* is, in turn, equated with the Mandate of Heaven (T'ien-ming). A nature *(hsing)* derived from the Mandate of Heaven does not solely consist of abstract human nature. Rather, it pertains to the actual nature of a person, what is called characteristics. Among Sung

Dynasty Idealists, this is called the nature of *ch'i* and *chih* (material force and material principle). Principle and material force unite to form the nature of a person. An abstract nature is limited by material force (*ch'i*) owing to differences in the clarity or turbidity of each individual. When asked by students why different persons possess material force (*ch'i*) in different way, Chu Hsi himself could not give an answer. Actually, this is what the Chinese often call "fate" or Mandate of Heaven. In Scholastic philosophy, characteristics are derived from "prime matter", which limits form. Body limits the soul, in this way leading to different talents and characteristics in different individuals. Characteristics are quantifiable. However, the soul is the foundation of life. If one's characteristics are derived from the body, then, after death, whereupon the soul separated from the body, the soul loses its limitation, which would then mean that all souls are undifferentiated. Furthermore, angels possess no corporeal body. They only have souls. If the soul is not limited, then angels would also be undifferentiated. Both of these are absurd. We then must say: God created the soul of each one based on his own idea, which differs from person to person. Thus, the created souls are themselves differentiated from one another. After the union of body and soul, the soul limits the body. Thus, a certain type of soul will lead to a certain type of body. Ancient Chinese philosophers, such as Chang Tsai and Wang Ch'uan-shan, proposed that man's characteristics result from the interplay of *yin* and *yang, and the Five Agents according to the Mandate of Heaven.*

II. Living Realities

After generation, each thing exists independently to become an existent reality. An existent reality is an integral, actual thing. When a person exists, the existing substance is this very person, or this very "ego." "Ego" exists. It is an existenet substance. However, when the ego exists, it does not follow that the ego is the substance and its existence an accident, or that existence is the ego's existence. Instead, the ego is itself existence and existence is the ego. Without existence, then there would not be ego. If there is ego, then ego exists. Réné Descartes said: " I think, therefore I am." This does not mean that I exist because

I think. Rather, I think, and therefore, I am a thinker. And this thinker is me. I, of course, exist. I exist. I am and existing person.

"Ego" is existence. The ego is a reality. A reality is an integrity. Scholastic philosophy differentiates between substance and accidents. A substance is a subsistent thing while accidents adhere to substance. This point can also be explained in terms of abstract theory. In actual terms, however, they are united and indivisible. In theory, a wooden table's substance is table, to which are added the accidents: wooden material, color and shape. In actual terms, wooden material is the substance of this table. Color and shape are this table's characteristics. They are indivisible from one another. If they are divided from one another, this table ceases becoming this table.

I am a person made up of body and soul. Soul possesses talents while body has its shape, size and color. All these joined together to make up "me". If any of them is separated, then I cease to be me. One does not need to separate the soul from the body or to separate the body's limbs. One only has to change my bodily size or skin color to make me cease from being me. I am an integral body, with substance and accidents undivided. These two can only be separated in an abstract way and in theory. In actual terms, they are inseparable.

The reason why a reality is "one" can be traced to "existence." " Existence" is the basis. "Existence' is one. Each reality can only have one existence. If a reality possesses dual or multiple existences, then it is not one reality but instead two or more realities. The substance and accidents of a reality both adhere is one "existence." Existence unites substance and accidents into one. I am one reality. My soul and body, and all the latter's parts, colors and shapes, all inhere in one existence. This one existence unites all of them to form an integral me.

"Existence" finds its realization in "nature". The existence of each thing is based on its "nature." For instance, man's existence finds realization in human nature. Similarly, my "existence" also finds its realization in my characteristics. Human nature is an abstract, theoretical nature. The nature of actual things are their characteristics. Nature (*hsing*) is derived from the Mandate of Heaven. It is the Creator's idea of creating things.

III. Existence is Life

The I *Ching* deals with changes in the universe. It says: "The successive movement of *yin* and *yang* consitutes the way (Tao)" (Chan 266). All changes result from the changes in *yin* and *yang*. These changes continue without ceasing. "What issues from the Way is good, and that which realizes it is individual nature" (Chan 266). The nature that results is one that changes, or a principle (*li*) that continues to change with the movement of *yin* and *yang*. The whole cosmos continuously undergoes changes as is the case with each thing in it. This is why Wang Ch'uan-shan said: "Life decreases while nature increases day by day." This immanent, continuous change is called life. The "Appended Remarks" says: "*I* (change) is the perpetual renewal of life" (Part 1, Chapter V). The ancient Chinese viewed the universe as a universe that changes with the annual four seasons. Growth spring. Maturity in summer. Harvest in fall. Storage in winter. This cycle continuously goes on. Every person, fowl, beast, blade of grass is perpetually undergoing change and living. The universe and the myriad things are all living things.

God is Pure Act. He is Absolute Life. He created the universe with his creative power. The universe is one living power, called "generative power." Generative power shares the creative ability of God's creative power. Thus, it generated the universe and all the myriad things. Within each thing it generated, generative power continues triggering further changes. Thus, each thing has continuous movement and life within itself. The act and manifestation of life are most perfect within man. Within the whole universe, man's life is the highest form of life. His is a psychophysical [2] life, a life characterized by spirituality.

---

(2) [Translator's note] Here, the term "psychophysical" should not be confused with its usage by Curt. J. Ducasse (1881-1969). Rather, it is borrowed to express the meaning of the original Chinese *hsin wu he-yi* 心物合一 , which means "the union of body and mind." The word sould also be interpreted as such in other parts of this translation.

The existence of each thing is a moving existence. It is always "act," or is always life. Life is activity. Activities of life are called "acts." The Pure Act did not lead from potency to act. It is Pure Act simpliciter. Therefore, change is not applicable to the Pure Act. It cannot have any new "act." The life of angels proceeds from potency to act. However, since angels are pure spiritual realities, they do not experience any corporeal change at all. On the contrary, man's life is a phsychophysical life, or a psychophysical existence. Therefore, the "act" of man's life leads from potency to act, which necessarily involves change. This is because man's body is material. If material objects have immanent activities, then they necessarily undergo quantitative change.

A person is an ego. Ego is existence. It is life. Since the existence of ego is life itself, then it is in act and always involves change. Physically, the ego constantly changes from birth to old age. The same is true with the ego's mind. The ego is a living reality. A change in life means a change in the reality, or a change in the ego itself. If the ego undergoes change, it is not the ego that changes, nor is it only the ego's body or color that changes. Instead, it is the ego itself that undergoes change.

Scholasticism, which adheres to the ideas of Aristotle, explains changes in the universe as either substantial or accidental. substantial change leads to either generation or annihilation. Accidental change is either quantitative change or qualitative change. Changes in each individual person are accidental changes.

Since changes involving life are all changes occurring in realities, and because realities are integral, then all changes occurring in a reality are changes in the whole reality. A reality is itself life. Are changes occurring in realities substantial or accidental? In the abstract, theoretical sense, they can be called accidental changes. However, they are actually changes occurring in the integral reality, which is one and indivisible. An integral unity is derived from "existence", which is itself "life" and arising from "life." Life is generative power. I live and I change. I change because of life which persists in every part of my wholeness, undifferentiated as substance or as accident. Each change that occurs arises from life, or is due to generative power. Each of these changes is a change in life, and is manifested in the different parts of my wholeness. Changes in me are changes in my life. They are changes occurring in my wholeness. Since changes occur in my wholeness, then why do I not turn into another "me" or immediately perish" The reason rests in the fact that life is one. The nature of my life is one. Life acts based on nature (*hsing*). I constantly live because the Mandate of Heaven (*T'ien-ming*) that is in my lives. And since the Mandate of Heaven is one, I then remain constantly as me.

I constantly remain "I." In terms of time, this is explained by the fact that life is "one." I am "existence", which is also life. Existence is one. I am also one. In terms of space, this is explained by the fact that all parts of my psychophysical whole still join together as an integral one owing to life. Life joins all my parts together. Any part which possesses no life does not belong to me.

Each thing remains one because of an immanent motive force, or generative power. Plants and animals also become one because of life. Similarly, minerals and rocks also remain one by virtue of this immanent motive force or generative power.

Existence is "act." "Act" is a nature immanent activity or life. The definition of life *per se* is "immanent self activity". God lives because of his immanent self activity. Besides, this activity is Pure Act, which is not derived from potency. Thus, in God, there is absolutely no change. All the myriad things in the universe possess corporeality. Since corporeality implies immanent self-activity, then changes occur in the myriad things with arise from the passage from potency to act. The life of the myriad things in the universe involves change, whose degree depends upon each thing's corporeality. Things are differentiated into categories, which, in turn, are made up of individuals. These classification and individuality are derived from the

Mandate of Heaven. The life acting within a mineral acts slowly owing to the mineral's high degree of corporeality. In comparison, plants possess a lighter degrees of corporeality, which explains why they manifest faster activities. Animals, who possess even lighter corporeality, are capable of even faster life activities. Man, who possesses a spiritual soul, has life activities that are both mysterious and unfathomable.

IV. Fulfillment of Nature

From the time of Confucius, traditional Chinese philosophy has always propounded the idea of self-cultivation and fulfilling of human nature. The *Ta Hsueh* (Great Learning) serves as the *vade mecum* of Neo-Confucian self-cultiviation. Chapter 1 of the *Ta Hsüeh* tells us the gist of the book. It reads: "The Ways (Tao) of learninig to be great consists in manifesting the clear character. It consists in caring for the people, so that they grow in talent and virtue everyday. It also consists in leading all people to the level of extreme good." The *Chung-yung* (Doctrine of the Mean) is the basis of the Neo-Confucian spiritual life. Chapter XXII of the *Chung-yung* deals with a person who attains utmost sincerity. It expounds on how such a person can fulfill his own charateristics in order to fulfill his own human nature, and then later, fulfill his corporeal nature to finally attain the level of praising the work of creation by Heaven and Earth. This highest level represents the fusion of the virtues of man and of Heaven.

Neo-Confucians do not believe that human nature is complete or fixed upon birth. Instead, they uphold that upon birth, a person possesses basic human nature, that is, the basic reasons and power to make man a man. In the words of Mencius, these are called the rudiments of benevolence, righteousness, propriety and wisdom. During his whole lifetime, man must exert efforts to cultivate his mind and his nature in such a way that he fulfills the goodness of human nature. Both Hsün-tzu and Chu Hsi believed that one becomes a sage after studying how to become a gentleman (*chun-tzu*). Wang Ch'uan-shan often dealt with his idea of "practising goodness such that it becomes part of one's nature."

In actual terms, human nature and characteristics are a packet of energy. For Mencius, spiritual and physical energy are called talents. This packet of energy must be actualized in the course of time. The life of the "ego" also includes this packed of energy. Life activities are themselves life, which in turn, is the exercise of this energy. From birth onwards, man's body grows everyday. Upon reaching maturity, however, it deteriorates following the weakening of his corporeality. Conversely, one's spiritual life continues to develop from childhood to old age, during which it wields all kinds of powers. In Western philosophy, intellectual life represents a person's life. It allows man's knowledge to gradually increase. The higher one's knowledge gets, the higher one's status becomes. In Chinese philosophy, one's emotional (feeling) life represents a person's life. It allows man's moral vitrues to grow day by day towards utmost goodness.

Human life is a phsychophysical life. The soul is the root of man's life, as well as its master. Activities of man's spiritual life necessarily possess principles and objectives. The soul is spiritual. The principles of spiritual activities are themselves the principles of morality while the objective of spiritual activities is the enjoyment of absolute truth, beauty and goodness. Thus, Hegel once proposed man's return to the absolute spirit through spiritual philosophy, which consists in the search for beauty, goodness and truth through art, religion and philosophy. Prof. Thome Fang once called a person who has reached a transcendent level as "a man of arts, ethics and religion." A life characterized by search for truth, beauty and goodness does not consist in the accumulation of external knowledge and good habits. Rather, it entails fulfillment of one's own characteristics and the realization of one's own life. The search for true knowledge and beautiful impressions is related to things outside one's self. Their possession benefits the spirit. The search for goodness by the cultivation of virtues consists in the accumulation of good habits. Habits are external forms whose contents mean the development of life. Therefore, only when the fruits of the search for beauty and truth are fused with moral principles can they really lead to the development of life. In actual terms, the development of one's spiritual life is itself the acquisition of moral virtues. "Practising goodness such that it becomes part of one's nature" makes the ego's character gradually fulfilled. The Gospel of St. Luke rocords that incident when the twelve-year-old Jesus returned from Jerusalem to Nazareth: "And Jesus increased in wisdom, in stature, and in favor with God and men" (Lk. 2:52). Ancient theologians and Bible experts considered Jesus Christ as both man and God. Right from birth, He possessed divine virtues and wisdom, which needed no improvement. For them, St. Luke's "increased" must be interpreted as an external manifestation. Contemporary Bible scholars and theologians believe that Jesus Christ is both man and God, and possessing real human nature. In his life as man, He totally lived the life of humans following natural principles. His wisdom and virtues gradually increased in the right sense of the word as used by St. Luke. The human character of Jesus also grew gradually.

V. Consciousness

Consciousness is the ego's self knowledge of its own existence and action. The consciousness of spiritual beings is a type of "clear vision" (*ming-chien*). Spiritual beings, possessing a clear substance, see their own selves and other spiritual beings by clear vision, which is both direct and penetrating. Man is a psychophysical being. His soul is spiritual. According to Hsün-tzu, the mind (soul) is a vacuous spirit while the body is material in nature and whose substance does not possess clarity. Human life is a psychophysical life. Thus, activities of the soul are performed through the body. Similarly, activities of the body also depend on the soul. Therefore, man does not have a clear vision of knowledge. Instead, man needs the body's nervous and sensory organs in order to know.

Réné Descartes said: "I think, therefore I am." The ego's knowledge of its own existence is intuitive. It cannot be proven and, in fact, need not be proven. For the ego, it exists because it lives. The ego is living. What lives is the ego. The ego's consciousness of its own existence is intuitive. It is the foundation all of his knowledge.

Physiological life is the first type of the ego's life. It is the process of the body's growth, which is the first part of the ego's life. Physiological life uses all the ego's bodily organs. To know or to be conscious of this life, use of the ego's sensory organs is necessary. The sensory organs, however, cannot have a vision of themselves. Thus, they cannot have a consciousness of the body's physiological life.

Sensitive life is one the body's corporeal lives. However, for senses to become sense knowledge, they must first pass through spiritual knowledge. This is so because the mind (soul) sees itself. It is conscious of bodily senses.

The life of the mind is a type of spiritual life. However, mental activities requires the use of the nervous system, which is corporeal in nature. The ego is not capable of having a "clear vision" of the life of the mind. It can only have consciousness. Knowing is an activity belonging to the ego. By introspection, the ego further knows the subject known.

When the ego lives, it remains conscious of its existence and its activities. It is the spiritual life viewing itself. Because the ego is psychophysical being, the soul must see itself through the body, and thus, it can only have intuition and introspection.

There is another type of consciousness belonging to spiritual life. The development of spiritual life tends towards the search for truth, beauty and goodness. Truth, beauty and goodness are infinite. Thus, the objectives of spiritual life are likewise infinite. And because of this, the development of spiritual life is also infinite. Nothing in man's life can satisfy this search, a fact that leads to man's feeling of dissatisfaction. Justice is regulated by spiritual life. The human world is full of injustice. Retribution between good and evil always leads to man's feeling of frustration and confusion. Because of man's infinite search, the full attainment of justice makes man's life acquire an enternal consciousness aimed at the fulfillment of the objectives of life.

Different lives also possess a joint consciousness. All life in the universe joins into one. All created things are interconnected. This connection is not existential connection. The living realities are each independent realities. They are interconnected by the need to develop their lives. In terms of its substance, life is generative power. The universe and generative power are one. Each thing is also formed by the one, same generative power. This generative power can only perform its activities if the generative power of each thing joins with the generative power of the universe and later, with the Creator's creative power. Only is this way can God's continual creation be made possible.

The ego's life shares the divine creative power's generative and creative powers. Thus, the ego's life acquires a creative quality and a generative ability. The ego's life can generate another ego. It can create other things, works of art, literary works and other things.

The life of the ego is totally intertwined with the whole universe, even with eternity.

Works Cited

Chan, Wing-tsit. *A Source Book in Chinese* Philosophy. Princeton: Princeton, UP, 1963.

(Translated by: Carols G. Tee)